ERIC NEWTON AND GRAHAM HANDLEY

A guide to teaching poetry

UNIVERSITY OF LONDON PRESS LTD

ISBN 0 340 11799 Unibook

University of London Press Ltd
St Paul's House, Warwick Lane, London EC4
Printed and bound in Great Britain by
Richard Clay (The Chaucer Press) Ltd.
Bungay, Suffolk

Contents

Acknowledgments

We and the publishers would like to thank the following for permission to reprint poems quoted in the text: The Literary Trustees of Walter de la Mare and the Society of Authors as their representative for *At the Keyhole* and *The Fly*; Norman McCaig and the Hogarth Press Ltd for *Granton* from *MEASURES*; Christopher Leach for *Blackbird*; Edith Scovell and the Cresset Press Ltd for *Boy Fishing*; James Reeves and Messrs Heinemann Ltd for *Slowly* and *The Sea* from *THE WANDERING MOON*; David Shavreen for *The Wind at Night* and *The Fair*; Max Flisher and Brooke Bond Ltd, for poems by Diane Martin, Richard Gray, Gerald Berkley, Julie Floyd, David Morrison, Bruce MacRae, Margaret Still and David Pomroy; Jennifer Noble for *Mongol*, Sylvia Huggler who printed this poem in 'Poems for Children', Thomas Blackburn, editor of *PRESENTING POETRY* and Messrs Methuen Ltd, publishers of this book, in which the chapter occurs; Mrs D. Ellenberg for Gabriel Ellenberg's *Skull of a Dead Bird*; Mrs. Bertelli for Philip Bertelli's *New York City*; Mr Thirsk, of Highlands Junior School, Ilford for *Drops on a Stone* and *Candlelight*; Mr Head and Miss Stirling of Poole's Park Junior School for *P.E.*, *Bargains* and *Shoes*; the House Governor of Chetham School, Manchester, H. Vickers and the Senior English Master, T. D. Gamson, for poems by Anthony Harpur, John Moon and Thomas Clough.

We are particularly grateful to a number of colleagues and friends who have assisted us in the preparation of this book. We feel we should mention by name Cecile Covill, Liz Farrer, Norman Hidden and Max Flisher, who have helped us with advice and material. Many of our students have underlined for us the need for our approach, and have demonstrated by their own imagination and drive that *young* ideas are very much in the process of shooting. Two teachers, Pauline Stapleton and Janet Green, have allowed us to use poems written in their classes, while above we make formal acknowledgments wherever we have been able to trace the author, no easy task in the case of some of the children who are often merely remembered as David or Shirley. Lastly, no acknowledgment is sufficient to convey our debt to the encouragement of Sylvia Huggler; this book could be dedicated to no one but her.

ERIC NEWTON AND GRAHAM HANDLEY

FOR SYLVIA

Introduction

THIS book needs little explanation by way of an introduction. It is what its title suggests, a guide for those many teachers and teachers in training who find themselves confronted by a poem and a number of indifferent or expectant eyes as they begin to read it. Sometimes, indeed, the reader may find a distinct hostility against the reading of a poem, a this-is-a-waste-of-time attitude, particularly at the secondary stage.

The reading of a poem, the experience and response of both reader and listener, can be one of the most intimate and enriching fulfilments of the many which teaching has to offer; yet large numbers of teachers and student teachers either scorn or are apprehensive about what should be the central delight of communication with their pupils. Poetry is not to be feared, nor is it to be denigrated, nor is it to be omitted altogether because of the 'built-in' resistance of tough boys or the romantic predilections of precocious girls. Poetry is at once a challenge and a surrender, for in reading it we give a vital part of ourselves to the experience, and in listening, we give a vital part of ourselves to the response. And just as improvisation in drama, or any dramatic expression for that matter, is an extension or deepening of experience, so is poetry, whether it gives rise to an activity, a discussion, or merely sets the reader thinking and examining, perhaps beginning to see an idea or an object with new eyes and new associations. The words of a poem are seeds which germinate in other minds and, for many readers, once the process of germination has begun, the harvesting continues throughout life.

In their own time teachers should read as much poetry as they can, and it should in the main be adult poetry which will deepen their inward lives and consequently the lives of those they teach. This will mean discarding at the outset any preconceived ideas of what poetry is or should be, and it will certainly mean ignoring literary jargon, an alien language to more than ninety per cent of our children anyway. It will lead to an ability to discuss poetry with children frankly, directly, imaginatively, without using the archaisms and definitions which, in the past, have reduced poetry to a formal exercise rather than a living experience. We, as teachers, must aim at capturing and transmitting the essential quality and spirit of the poems we teach, and this means much practice in reading aloud to ourselves as well as in silent exploration.

For each teacher the manner of presentation of a poem will be different, just as our many interpretations of the same poem are different in quality and degree. Do not cheapen a child's appreciation by a diet of poetry which makes no demands on him either intellectually or emotionally; he is already familiar with a world whose horizons are limited to 'pop' as a desired and desirable substitute for living. What we are all trying to do is to educate our children in the spirit as well as the mind, and this means that we shall constantly revert, though perhaps not overtly in our teaching, to the moral context in which we all live.

Through poetry which explores a multiplicity of situations and attitudes, a child's moral awareness may be quickened and sustained; the poem which describes violence may even act as an antidote against the violence of the television screen – which often carries no commentary – or the violence which is reported sensationally in the press, with its overtones of glamour. Not all the poetry you teach will have this serious import. Much of it will be light and fresh, attractive at once to the ear and the inward eye, perhaps humorous, whimsical, fantastic. Its range is the range of life experience, and the good teacher will bring to her pupils as much of that range as she – and they – can encompass.

The method of presentation in this book is one of sequence and gradual development, so that you will not find all that you require in one chapter, but as the approach in each chapter is largely the same, you will find a degree of overlapping. In most sections our aim is to look closely – and to help you to look closely – at individual poems. Generally this look takes the form of a specific commentary or suggestions for activity. The chapter headings are, therefore, guidelines to an investigation; that investigation is yours as well as ours, and its paramount aim is to make the nature of poetry a vital part of each teacher's consciousness.

I

Poetry and the Teacher

IT is our aim in this chapter to establish common ground in the teacher's approach to poetry and her own appreciation at an adult level. For many this will mean a fundamentally new appraisal, and here it must be re-emphasized that the approach should not be based on the comprehension and figures-of-speech catalogue which many teachers still find so convenient and which is certainly the least arduous way of measuring 'appreciation'.

The teacher's approach should evolve from her own intelligent and sensitive responses to language and her own emotional reactions to the poetry she reads. Here there is assuredly common ground with the way in which we expect young children to react to poetry; as Marie Peel has rightly observed,

> children delight in the directness of poetry, its sharp exact appeal to the senses, which makes the poet's world, if he is a good poet, strangely akin to their own : all presentation and *outsight*, no analysis. There is often an explosive, magical quality. (*Seeing to the Heart*, p. 29.)

Analysis as commonly practised for examination purposes is rightly condemned too for the adult, but there are criteria by which a poem may in part be judged, though there is no rule-of-thumb procedure for the evaluation of poetry. Each poem is in the nature of an experience in which the senses and the intellect are usually involved; with all good poetry, indeed, they are involved at one and the same time. With mathematics or a foreign language the eye and the ear may delight in pattern or sound, but the direct and immediate involvement is with the mind; the emphasis is on logical facts, sequences or sets of rules which establish the basis of understanding or relating or deduction. But poetry is subject to no rules, for though it can be measured in terms of rhyme and rhythm, figures of speech and alliteration, and it has its own dictionary of technical terms, the immediacy of its appeal and the associations which that appeal sets up cannot simply be categorized or labelled.

It is important, therefore, that the teacher who finds herself out of sympathy with the literary jargon which still unfortunately passes for appreciation with some of our examining bodies, should not be deterred from reading, enjoying and then *teaching* poetry. She should read each poem with the eye of her imagination and the ear of her heart and, unknown to herself, she may start with the inestimable advantage of discovering that she need not milk poetry for its literal meaning.

Obviously, the teacher needs to give some time to her own exploration of poetry, and here we must reassert our belief that much contemporary verse carries its own rewards for teacher and child alike. As Marie Peel says:

> The writers of one's own time speak more immediately and intimately to most people than those of earlier periods, no matter how great. Even more important, they sometimes speak *for* us. Their concerns are often peculiarly our concerns. Also our experience of our own time makes us able to judge the genuineness of an author's awareness in a way that we cannot do with earlier writers without very extensive knowledge of the period, and not only of its literature ... (*Seeing to the Heart*, p. 24.)

At adult level much modern poetry is available in reasonably cheap paperback editions, and these may contain one or two poems suitable for children as well (see the bibliography at the end of the book for a list which should prove useful). Occasionally, small poetry magazines repay browsing time. In addition, Penguin Books are in the process of publishing much modern poetry in translation, and we have found this a rich storehouse of material, some of which the teacher will find eminently suitable for reading to upper primary and secondary school children.

It is not always easy to determine whether some contemporary poetry is true poetry or not. But our senses may have been dulled by memories of the kind which Alison Edmonds feelingly describes in *Presenting Poetry* where she refers to the child's dislike of the 'poetry lesson' – formal, stilted, divorced from experience – and of the vast majority of anthologies which were provided for children in the past. Both, she suggests, were the result of what she calls 'adult expedience', and the practice was to work through the poems of 'long-dead writers'; the result, inevitably, was 'excruciating boredom'.

As Robert Druce says (in *The Eye of Innocence*) poetry is not 'bogus Wordsworth' or 'synthetic Keats', or 'e'er, o'er, 'twas and wert'; he then tells us exactly what it is:

> It is writing that is at a higher emotional pitch than normal; it is the heightened awareness of the world in at least one of its aspects. It is a statement of the 'truths that lie waiting in all things' ... For all this is language drawn at a venture, newly-minted, exuberant, spendthrift. (*The Eye of Innocence*, pp. 26–7.)

This is the authentic voice of enthusiasm, and it is enthusiasm – not brash, not salesman-like, not superficial – that the teacher of poetry must possess. It is enthusiasm in the infectious sense of the word, synonymous with the love, the joy, the certainty, the unique freshness of discovery.

In choosing poetry for herself and for her children, the teacher must read and read widely. Obviously she should include traditional material which seems to her to embody valid imaginative or narrative qualities which could make it an experience for teacher and class alike. Generally, the poems she elects to teach should extend her as well as the children, whether the extension be a widening of experience, a deepening of self-knowledge, the description or presentation of a new aspect, or a vibrant moral or spiritual appraisal.

The teacher of poetry should try to avoid assuming the posture of a literary critic, whose intellectual discipline and measured treatment of what she reads often kill natural response; she should respond to the immediacy of the language, its associations, emphases, suggestions, sounds. She must build her own sensitivity and awareness by a constant exposure to the kindling power of poetry. To do this, over a period of time, is to become aware of, say, the difference in quality of the war poetry of Wilfred Owen on the one hand and that of Rupert Brooke on the other. Such awareness carries within itself the ability to evaluate in the true sense; to see the psychological realism, intensity and suffering of Owen against the overt patriotism, romanticism, but essentially less potent verse of Brooke.

The following poem (quoted in *Presenting Poetry* edited by Thomas Blackburn) was written by a child, but it demonstrates at once the singular conciseness of poetry, the heightened emotional intimacy established between writer and reader; anyone still unsure of the nature of poetry might consider, after reading this, how much would be lost if the simple statements were made in prose:

THE MONGOL · Jennifer Noble, aged 14–15

As he passes by they look away,
They look over his shoulder,
They stare at the sky,
Or an empty window,
Anywhere as long as their eyes don't meet his.

The tiny children run ahead and stare,
And poke out their tongues,
And waggle their fingers,
And grin, and giggle,
And then run in fear to their parents when he
Only grins back.

His 'friends', the eight-year-olds, walk beside him,
And hug his coat,
And say 'Hello' politely,
And give him sweets,
And then stand back sniggering in a corner as
He walks on.

The young wives turn away,
And clutch their children's hands,
And pet them,
And fuss them,
And don't smack them that morning.
Thankful that their minds fit their bodies so well.

High in his glasshouse the young executive looks down,
He sees the clumsy bulk in the gaberdine raincoat,

And fingers his Savile Row suit,
And fumbles between the telephone,
And the dictaphone,
And the linguaphone,
And remembers when he kicked him in school for
Not understanding the game.
And snaps at his secretary.

The few who treat him as a neighbour and a friend
Smile over-jovially,
Laugh too heartily,
Wave too energetically,
And sigh with awkward relief when they leave.

And the rest stare at him, or away, with pity, or regret,
And he holds his mother's hand,
And shoots the windows with his water-pistol,
And laughs at the sun,
And smiles at his friendly world.

This poem, written by a B-stream girl in a grammar school, possesses in the quality of its content and treatment, what A. E. Housman once referred to as 'the name and nature of poetry'. It reveals at once the paradox which is in each and every one of us, the reflexes of cruelty and compassion which are ours in varying and unpredictable degrees. With one shift of the imagination we see into the mind of the 'young executive' who represents the world of hard and fast reality in which *this* child can have no place. The switch of focus to this outside world may be considered crude, but it is none the less effective. It makes us only too keenly aware of the unequal nature of the individual lot in life. You don't need to be trained in rudimentary 'literary' appreciation to gain something from this poem. Admittedly, you need to be sensitive and responsive to language (notice the 'machines' in the office as compared with the 'clumsy bulk' of humanity), and perhaps you ought to have some awareness of the social, psychological and basically human problems which exist in our society.

This poem is conceived throughout in basically human terms, and it is a strongly individual, sympathetic statement, an imaginative extension of a special case seen through the eyes of one sensi-

B

tive person, and that person a child possessed, you may feel, of exceptional maturity and insight. Yet one senses that if this poem were read to a group of, say, thirteen-year-olds, it would evoke a more immediate and positive response than many of the formal and dated poems which still constitute the main content of a large number of our 'successful' anthologies.

Certainly *The Mongol* makes more demands in terms of personal involvement than nonsense verses or conventional poems about highwaymen. Children are notoriously suspicious of sentimentality, but it is precisely because of this that we should not be deterred from reading poetry which teacher and class alike may find moving, disturbing, distasteful or embarrassing, as well as poems which exalt in a spiritual, aesthetic or moral way or which are purely descriptive or narrative and without (apparent) overtones. In view of the undoubted influence of the mass media like television on young viewers – our young readers – the presentation of the human situation, as in the above poem, in a moral context is all the more important. The teacher who responds to this poem because of the human awareness which it displays is the more likely to provide her class with the stimulus to meaningful discussions of the problems faced by many of their mentally, socially or even racially less-privileged companions today. Poetry is often the initial impetus to increased understanding, tolerance and compassion for teacher and child.

The 'presentation of poetry' is a wide term covering, in the first place, the reading, re-reading and incidental reference in the classroom. For most children the quality of the teacher's presentation will determine the degree of acceptance and eventual love for poetry and the desire to read more. Unfortunately, many adults read poorly, consequently mutilating instead of enhancing the quality of the poet's thought, emotion or technical skill. In the classroom a poem has to make a prompt appeal to the ear, and it must not be thrown away; here the teacher who has established a positive relationship with her class should be able to communicate with them on a meaningful, stimulating perhaps humorous or even emotional (though not sentimental) level. Such communication is dependent on the teacher's use of her own voice.

But this is not to suggest that the royal road to teaching poetry is through elocution exercises. Practice in reading aloud there must be, but the first stage is through the silent contemplation of each poem, together with a consideration of what the poet is trying to say and how the poem *sounds* in one's *mind*. To *feel* the poem with one's imagination and senses alert and receptive is essential for most students and this, with some preparation of each poem to be read aloud, is all that is required.

Next, the teacher must set out to master the art of promoting class discussion and encouraging it without dominating. The evaluation of poetry through group discussion is normally part of the English course in colleges of education; the tutor seeks to draw forth the responses to what has been read based on both a human and an intelligent-cum-intellectual appraisal. The discussions may range far from the poem itself, but inevitably there will be exploration of some facet of the human situation.

The teacher in this workshop context (a context more fully set out in the following chapter), is in much the same position as the tutor with his group. The discussion may be informed in part by the quality of the teacher's response and knowledge, but its aim is surely to assist in educating the feelings and the minds of each variously different individual. It is more than possible that children who discuss poetry will, if encouraged, write poetry; obviously the teacher should take an interest in poetry for children, some poems for the youngest being well worth studying in depth. Ultimately they will help, though this is not stressed, in the evaluation of quality in children's own writing.

Some poetry for children, then, however simple it may at first appear, can contribute to the developing quality of the teacher's own imagination, and the more this happens the more she will communicate with and stir the imaginations of her pupils. She must look closely and perceptively at what she reads, for though every poem she reads may not be a joy, each one will certainly be a challenge.

Below we give an example of a poem which could be read and appreciated at both adult and child level; our appraisal of it is no more than a guide towards the teacher's approach. The sensitive, responsive reader will fill in our omissions by the quality of her own imaginative reading; something of that quality – and remember that each individual response is different – will rub off on to her pupils, and they in their turn will discover something new about themselves, or about life or a facet of life, or at least about the subject of the poem, from their own reactions:

THE FLY · Walter de la Mare

How large unto the tiny fly
  Must little things appear!
A rosebud like a feather bed,
  Its prickle like a spear.

A dewdrop like a looking-glass,
  A hair like golden wire;
The smallest grain of mustard-seed
  As fierce as coals of fire;

A loaf of bread, a lofty hill;
A wasp, a cruel leopard;
And specks of salt as bright to see
  As lambkins to a shepherd.

The adult reader will note that the poet establishes his perspective in the first two lines and then proceeds to illustrate it through a series of images; indeed, one can trace the logical development of his thought through this sequence of images. The poem falls into two sections; in the first we are outside in the garden on a summer's morning, while in the second we are inside at the meal-table. The objects of attention are selected for their contrasts as well as their associations.

The sequence is logical, from the rosebud to the prickle, next to each other, but contrasted in shape, colour and texture, as well as in the suggestions of rest and aggression which are evoked by the bed and the spear. The dewdrop and the hair are again contrasted in shape and texture, the one being of ephemeral quality while the other is permanent. Then there is the mustard seed, containing in its very being the paradox of size in relation to power. (Compare the biblical parable where the power lies in the tiny seed's capacity to grow.) Here it is the latent energy, derived from the sun, which causes it to burn 'as fierce as coals of fire'. Moreover, the images are inseparable from the sounds; the rhythms and the weight of the words or phrases change subtly as we listen to the first verse, beginning with the soft sounding consonants in 'feather' in contrast to the hard explosive sound of the word 'prickle'.

In the final verse one could likewise note shape, colour and luminescence in the objects chosen, but here, in contradistinction to the first section, we find a unity, a logical development in the form of a journey which could be regarded as a miniature after the pattern of so many of our folk tales. The loaf of bread is a hill (with the suggestion of aspiration and struggle); the wasp, the forces of danger on the road; and, when the summit is reached, the vision of safety, the green pastures of the psalmist, are epitomized by the lambs and the good shepherd.

As with any poem that comes 'trippingly on the tongue', the natural speech rhythms carry the shades of feeling and meaning – in fact the two are inseparable. One notices, too, that in every line the natural break comes in a different place, for example:

> *A loaf of bread / a lofty hill;*
> *A wasp / a cruel leopard;*

And this is consonant with the feeling which informs every verse. Here the sustained effort visualized in the first line is conveyed by the longer phrases, whereas a sudden, menacing impact is achieved by the earlier break in the second line. This throws into relief the phrase 'And specks of salt as bright to see' which dances and sparkles more brightly if the metrical structure is more strictly observed. On the other hand, 'lambkins' and 'shepherd' stand out best as complementary images if the first syllable of each word is gently emphasized almost at the expense of the other syllables.

Such a detailed exploration as we have undertaken here is not meant to suggest that other short poems should be subjected to similar consideration before they are read to children. This would be an impractical and often an unwise course anyway. Any analysis should be one of feeling rather than of technique. What is suggested is that some of the more sensitive children's poems, even those for the youngest, will reveal further depths of meaning as one gets to know them more intimately. As teachers of poetry to young children it is essential that we make a few of these poems a part of ourselves, a part which can be readily recalled and put to use in a moment. We will, of course, have a nodding acquaintance, perhaps something more, with a wide range of poems, but knowing a few intimately is integral to our responsibility to the children we teach. We have already stressed how greatly the experience of poetry at depth contributes to our development as individuals; the stimulus to experience, like the stimulus to play or work or create, can at best be shared with or at least fostered in our children.

Traditionally, after the manner of many primary school anthologies, poems have been defined by being labelled as 'humorous verse', 'nature poetry' and so on; but this is to run the risk of misunderstanding the essence of poetic quality. We can only generalize by saying that often poetry appeals most poignantly to the *ear* in the first instance or that it registers more immediately with the feelings than the intellect on first reading. But although a poem need not be fitted, and often cannot be fitted, into a particular category, it is perhaps useful for our purpose here to consider some of the many ingredients which give poetry its power to stimulate us in a way unique to itself.

The examples below have been chosen from well-known children's poems because they are readily available in a number of traditional anthologies. Perhaps we should give pride of place to the ingredient of *humour*, if only to correct the impression that poetry should be solemn or profoundly introspective or prettily descriptive. Nursery rhymes and folk poetry are often rich in humour, and Lewis Carroll and Edward Lear, to take the best-known writers of so-called 'nonsense', have established a tradition which teachers and children alike find endearing. But it is not only the inspired incongruity of their creations, the Jumblies, the Quangle-Wangle, the Pobble and the rest, which capture our attention. They are also memorable because of the haunting, musical quality of some of the lines:

> *Far and few, far and few,*
> *Are the lands where the Jumblies live;*
> *Their heads are green and their hands are blue,*
> *And they went to sea in a sieve.*

Edward Lear

or:

> *Calico Pie,*
> *The little birds fly*
> *Down to the calico tree.*
> *Their wings were blue,*
> *And they sang 'Tilly-loo'—*
> *Till away they flew,*
> *And they never came back to me,*

They never came back,
They never came back,
They never came back to me.

Edward Lear

The magic to be found in some of the children's poems of Walter de la Mare is of a different kind. Deeply rooted in ancient mythology and folk-lore, they awaken intuitive responses to the fears and longings which are legacies from our remotest ancestors. In the well-known *Silver* the moon is the ancient enchantress, and silver the symbol of her power. She, and only she, is moving; everything else is stilled, transmuted under her spell:

Slowly, silently, now the moon
Walks the night in her silver shoon.

Again, the magic may derive from ancient tales of giants and incantations to ward off the dark forces of evil.

These forces are clearly present in the next poem, all the more powerful for being insubstantial, as in 'a sheet webbed over my candle'. It is unnecessary to try to rationalize the forces. The poet gives form to the nameless terrors we all experience at times. They are there in the shadows of the room and, what is more, we feel that the Cobbler and Susie are part of this supernatural world and not merely visited by its powers. The words 'Grill me some bones' become a sinister echo of the giant's threat, 'I'll grind his bones to make my bread!':

AT THE KEYHOLE · Walter de la Mare

'Grill me some bones' said the Cobbler,
  'Some bones, my pretty Sue;
I'm tired of my lonesome with heels and soles,
Springsides and uppers too;
A mouse in the wainscot is nibbling;
A wind in the keyhole drones;
And a sheet webbed over my candle, Susie! —
  Grill me some bones!'

'Grill me some bones,' said the Cobbler,
  'I sat at my tic-tac-to;

And a footstep came to my door and stopped,
And a hand groped to and fro;
And I peered up over my boot and last;
And my feet went cold as stones –
I saw an eye at the keyhole, Susie! –
*   Grill me some bones!'*

A re-reading, hearing the sound of the lines in our own minds as we would wish to hear them spoken aloud, may suggest the question, 'How far does a child need to *understand* a poem?' To understand in the sense of finding a reasoned explanation of the poem may be irrelevant or indeed impossible; or perhaps, as the Plowden Report puts it, 'We recognize that children can grasp poetically what they cannot grasp intellectually.' Thus the time-honoured practice of oral testing for comprehension can in some cases be destructive to the nature of poetry. Some questions may arise, but it is better that they should come from the children, and then perhaps it is best to turn them back to the class. 'What do *you* think?' is sometimes a good question. Talk about the poetry by all means, but talk *with* the children, bearing in mind that the object of such talk is to awaken the children's own responses to the poet's feelings.

The poet, no less than the child, is concerned with the real world as well as the world of the imagination; but, like the child, he often makes no hard and fast distinctions between realism and fancy. John Clare (1793–1864) was very close to the natural world of his own countryside because he looked minutely and with imagination at what he saw around him. He was often preoccupied, as in the following poem, with tiny living and growing things and, by bringing them physically closer, he achieved a kind of identity with them. In *Clock-a-clay* he sees a small area of the natural world, as it were, on the level of its own existence.

CLOCK-A-CLAY · John Clare

In the cowslip pips I lie,
Hidden from the buzzing fly,
While green grass beneath me lies,
Pearled with dew like fishes' eyes,
Here I lie, a clock-a-clay,
Waiting for the time of day.

While grassy forest quakes surprise,
And the wild wind sobs and sighs,
My gold home rocks as like to fall,
On its pillar green and tall;
When the parting rain drives by
Clock-a-clay keeps warm and dry.

Day by day and night by night,
All the week I hide from sight;
In the cowslip pips I lie,
In rain and dew still warm and dry;
Day and night, and night and day,
Red, black-spotted clock-a-clay.

My home shakes in wind and showers,
Pale green pillar topped with flowers,
Bending at the wild wind's breath,
Till I touch the grass beneath;
Here I live, lone clock-a-clay,
Watching for the time of day.

The children will need to be told that clock-a-clay is a ladybird, of course, but otherwise their own direct observation should be more valuable than explanations by the teacher, who will be wise to draw from them what they have noticed. We cannot always have the real thing or even a picture at hand whenever we read a poem of this kind, but we should draw on the children's own experience even as we seek to extend it. The special qualities of Clare's poetry will be the better appreciated because of the frequent opportunities it gives for making close observation of living and growing things.

Young children's interest in living creatures evokes a response to animal poems of all kinds. Many children are stirred to strong compassion by poems which deal with hunting or trapping of creatures for sport or profit:

I hear a sudden cry of pain!
There is a rabbit in a snare;
Now I hear the cry again,
But I cannot tell from where.

James Stephens

On the other hand, in the experience of growing up children learn that the relationship with their pets is not merely the simple one of possessing without responsibility. To lavish affection may not be enough :

> I had a dove and the sweet dove died;
>   And I have thought it died with grieving:
> O, what could it grieve for? Its feet were tied,
>   With a silken thread of my hand's own weaving.
>
> John Keats

Here we have only had space to deal with one or two broad categories of poetry; obviously it covers many other subjects, in many moods, having both a universal and particular appeal. In this chapter we have tried to define poetry and to display its unique quality, at the same time showing how close it is in essence to the imagination and often the experience of children. The teacher of poetry cannot afford to let her own imagination slip, or indeed to lose her appetite for a life of sensations *and* thoughts; for children come to poetry as they come initially to all things, fresh, without the inhibitions of adulthood. The kindling of their imaginations, the stimulus to meaningful thought and activity, are the responsibility of the teacher; and in many cases the teacher, and the teacher alone, gives meaning and joy to the inward life which sustains and makes bearable the daily round of the commonplace.

2

Pre-school Language and Poetry

BEFORE we consider poetry in relation to the school child, we must recognize that the seeds of appreciation are sown in early childhood. For many children – and they are the fortunate ones – poetry begins on mother's knee, and that is where language learning begins also. The child's first linguistic experience is in *listening* and *responding*.

Communication between the baby and its mother is one of mutual response – the mother reacting to the child's gestures and noises, the baby responding to the mother's words and facial expressions. Poetry begins with nursery rhymes, and these again are a shared experience. The mother involves the baby physically in movements which accentuate the rhythm of the verse. 'To market, to market, to buy a fat pig', or 'Ride a cock horse', for example, are chanted as baby is bounced up and down on mother's knee, and it is difficult to imagine the rhyme

> *Here we go up, up, up,*
> *Here we go down, down, down,*
> *Here we go backwards and forwards,*
> *And here we go round, round, round,*

unaccompanied by vigorous swinging or lifting movements in which the baby and his mother are, as it were, one.

The rhythmic movement and the sound are inseparable, though at first the individual words may have no specific meaning. But very soon the child learns to associate various parts of his body with different sound symbols – the hands, perhaps, in 'Pat-a-cake, pat-a-cake, baker's man', the fingers and toes in 'This little pig went to market'; though he cannot say the words, he recognizes them when they are spoken by his mother. At a later stage, 'pat-a-cake, pat-a-cake' may take on a new meaning as he watches his mother at work in the kitchen and, perhaps, relives the experience in his play.

The developing interests of the young child are reflected in the many nursery rhymes about everyday things the child can recognize, about other people and animals he may meet, about the sequence of going to bed, getting up in the morning, eating and dressing with which he is familiar, about the weather, his mother's work in the house and a number of other phenomena within his experience. Through familiarity with the rhymes he learns the words necessary to identify and classify many objects and living things he meets; thus he begins to bring a measure of order into the complex world which surrounds him.

Nursery rhymes are probably the best-known literature of the English-speaking world. People who have memorized little else can usually recite *Mary had a little lamb* or *Jack and Jill went up the hill*. The wide range of interest, appeal and sheer usefulness of the rhymes in school is, however, not always realized. Here are a few pointers which can be followed up by reading any handy collection, such as *The Puffin Book of Nursery Rhymes* (Iona and Peter Opie).

Ideally, the nursery rhymes provide the link in literature between the home and the child's first school, though their range is so extensive that we, as adults, never entirely grow out of them. Some rhymes, on a homely level, set out to teach sequences; even if this is not their primary purpose, they can certainly be used in this way in school :

> *Solomon Grundy,*
> *Born on* Monday ...

> January *brings the snow* ...

> One, two, *buckle my shoe* ...

Others have the fascination of growing in ever-widening circles of complexity, as in *This is the house that Jack built* ... or, by contrast, of gradualy diminishing to a single focal point, and then growing again to its original size, as in *This is the key of the kingdom* (see page 32). Some rhymes are in the form of question and answer dialogue, and can be used in the classroom for simple group speaking. Others have choruses or refrains (sometimes quite difficult to speak) in which all the children may join.

'Difficult' themes, such as *death* or *violence*, usually avoided in literature written for children, are generally acceptable in nursery rhymes. The stylized treatment can keep the experience at a distance or make it beautiful perhaps, without being frightening:

> *Who killed Cock Robin?*
> *I, said the Sparrow,*
> *With my bow and arrow,*
> * I killed Cock Robin.*

In any case, since children will be coping with their own fantasies of violence, it is better to bring the subject into the open. In fact, there are very few rhymes which are unacceptable, and the teacher would obviously omit those which have objectionable racial connotations or which are aimed, in a rather crude way, at frightening children into obedience.

Some of the tongue-twisters and the riddling or puzzle rhymes have an appeal which, in a light and amusing way, gives children confidence and respect for their own intellect. Other rhymes are full of compassion, particularly in their concern for the smaller, more helpless creatures:

> *The North Wind doth blow,*
> *And we shall have snow,*
> *And what will the Robin do then, poor thing?*

Many nursery rhymes have a wide vocabulary which makes no needless concessions to the child's understanding by talking down to him in the patronizing way that some of the stories in his 'readers' do. Yet, because the context is easily understood and synonyms are freely used, they present little difficulty. No child is likely to worry about the 'meaning' of

> *On a misty moisty morning,*
> *When cloudy was the weather,*
> *I met a little old man*
> *Clothed all in leather . . .*

or

> *This is the priest all shaven and shorn*
> *that married the man all tattered and torn*
> *that kissed the maiden all forlorn . . .*

In any case, poetry is 'understood' through the emotions as much as through the intellect, and few children would complain about not understanding a nursery rhyme.

Together with the fairy stories, the nursery rhymes provide a link and a nourishment for the child's imaginative life. Kings, queens, princes and princesses, giants, witches and talking animals, all have their individual characters which are always consistent with their prototypes. At the same time, everyday characters can be seen to do the most surprising things. Cats can make romantic journeys to 'see the Queen', old women go 'hippety-hop' or 'live in a shoe' and 'cows jump over the moon'. But some of the lines themselves have their own quality of magic which cannot be analysed. If, as W. H. Auden has said, poetry is 'memorable speech', then many lines from nursery rhymes would fit that definition:

> Rings on her fingers and bells on her toes
> And she shall have music wherever she goes.

> I had a little nut tree,
> Nothing would it bear
> But a silver nutmeg
> And a golden pear.

> Tom he was a piper's son,
> He learned to play when he was young,
> But the only tune that he could play
> Was 'Over the hills and far away'.

Nursery rhymes can be associated with other school activities, even with the youngest children. They are some of the children's first songs, and a collection of nursery rhymes may well be the first book that a child possesses. Iona and Peter Opie, in their preface to *The Puffin Book of Nursery Rhymes*, write:

> We would suggest that there are few books more attractive to a small child who wants to learn to read than a nursery rhyme book. He already knows a number of rhymes or parts of them, and he can gain confidence by pretending to read what he already knows. The illustrations guide him to the subject-matter, and when he has to guess a word the rhythm and rhyme are sometimes a powerful assistance.

But, of course, nursery rhymes are meant to be spoken aloud. Some are little more than jingles (though none the less useful for certain purposes). They just need clear and rhythmic speaking. Others call for something more than that if they are to make their maximum impact. It is always better not to let our familiarity with a poem blind us to the aesthetic quality of the words. We should try to read it as if for the first time; as if the language were newly minted. The choice of what to read is always a matter of importance, and whichever verses the discriminating teacher decides to make her own will be those likely to carry conviction with the children.

Even a nursery rhyme may call for an interpretation, and this implies 'speaking' rather than merely saying the verse. The particular interpretation chosen *must* preserve the prescribed pattern and structure of the verse; but within these limitations many variations are possible. Subtle alterations of pitch, pace, pause, volume, emphasis and rhythmic 'stretching' are possible even in a short poem. But what is possible may not be desirable. It is a matter of taste, and what one person may feel is a legitimate 'dramatic' interpretation, another may regard as one overloaded with 'expression'. The choice is the teacher's, and one can only generalize by saying that, in the first place, the reader's involvement (which is sometimes called 'sincerity') is essential and, in the second place, the children appreciate a teacher's obvious intention to convey the drama or 'spirit' of a poem. Let us take a simple example:

> *My mother said I never should*
> *Play with the gipsies in the wood;*
> *If I did, she would say,*
> *Naughty girl to disobey.*
> *Your hair shan't curl*
> *And your shoes shan't shine,*
> *You gipsy girl,*
> *You shan't be mine.*
>
> *And my father said that if I did*
> *He'd rap my head with a teapot-lid.*
> *The wood was dark; the grass was green;*
> *In came Sally with a tambourine.*
> *I went to the sea – no ship to get across;*

I paid ten shillings for a blind white horse;
I up on his back and was off in a crack,
Sally tell my mother I shall never come back.

There is a dark sense of mystery pervading the poem, but the mood changes at least twice. The fear of the unknown which haunts the little girl, the mysterious call of the gipsy and the eventual escape, are within the experience of us all, adults as well as children. If this is accepted and felt by the reader, it will affect the tone of voice, and indeed cast a spell on reader and listener alike. The first verse may be read with a sharply accentuated rhythm (it has an incantatory quality). The roughness of the father's utterance is amusing by contrast. But parental authority is meant to be flouted, if only in our dreams, and the mystery begins to build up until the child rides away into the unknown. Would we be dogmatic if we suggested that this final escape, not being a matter of *fact*, could be spoken with a diminuendo on the last line?

Sally tell my mother I shall never come back.

The *way* the children listen will show whether our choice of interpretation is justified. The question 'Did you like it?' is irrelevant, and when it is asked, the answers are often misleading. From our foregoing remarks, it will be gathered that we regard the interest in nursery rhymes as extending far beyond the infant school stage.

Our next example is a poem which is as stylized as a minuet or a Chinese painting. In this case, the interpretation is influenced as much by the form as by the meaning. The reader needs control of volume, tone and pace to achieve the effect of a gradual diminution of the images in the first half, and the converse effect in the second half:

This is the key of the kingdom;
In that kingdom is a city;
In that city is a town;
In that town is a street;
In that street there is a lane;
In that lane there is a yard;
In that yard there is a house;
In that house there waits a room;

In that room an empty bed;
On that bed there is a basket;
In that basket there are some flowers.

Flowers in a basket;
Basket on the bed;
Bed in the room;
Room in the house;
House in the yard;
Yard in the lane;
Lane in the street;
Street in the town;
Town in the city;
City in the kingdom –
This is the key of the kingdom.
  Of the kingdom this is the key.

Although the poem is far removed from reality, the reader must believe in it himself if it is to sound convincing. An ability to visualize the kingdom, the town, the street and so on, will help the reader to impart a sense of immediacy and reality.

What does the poem mean? What is the *key*, and what the *kingdom?* As far as the children are concerned, the question may not arise. Paul West, the author of *Words to a Deaf Daughter* (Gollancz) says of Mandy, the subject of the book:

> She has changed my attitude to language. In schools they deal with ossified words – there's a complete lack of physical emphasis. Students always want to know what a word *means* rather than getting caught up in the feeling of it. They should be taught to appreciate that language is a sensuous thing.

If questions do arise from the children one can attempt some sort of 'explanation', but it is better to give a tentative lead which may provide a growing point for the children's imagination. For example one might say, 'Well, I suppose the poem is about a kind of journey. It starts in the *kingdom* ...'. Or, perhaps, 'What do we do with a *key?*' 'Yes, unlock doors, or boxes ... Can we unlock mysteries? ... or secrets? ...' The question which could be dismissed with a factual or one-word answer can be made to lead to the more

c

subtle question which extends meanings and leads to imaginative thinking.

Among traditional verses one can find many examples of sequential treatment. In *The Key of the Kingdom* one is reminded of the children's toy – a box within a box within a box ... In *A Man of Words* the sequences are apparently more inconsequential:

> *A man of words and not of deeds*
> *Is like a garden full of weeds;*
> *And when the weeds begin to grow,*
> *It's like a garden full of snow;*
> *And when the snow begins to fall,*
> *It's like a bird upon a wall;*
> *And when the bird away does fly,*
> *It's like an eagle in the sky;*
> *And when the sky begins to roar,*
> *It's like a lion at the door;*
> *And when the door begins to crack,*
> *It's like a stick across your back;*
> *And when your back begins to smart,*
> *It's like a penknife in your heart;*
> *And when your heart begins to bleed,*
> *You're dead and dead and dead indeed.*

In children's terms, if this is about anything it is about broken promises. On one level, they can understand that. But the poem has a darker meaning, mysterious and haunting. The *Man of Words* is alone in an alien world. The images themselves, menacing or hostile, may be rationalized at an adult level, but are not explicable to children. Yet this hardly matters. What *does* matter is that, having chosen to read the poem aloud, the reader is committed to create the appropriate atmosphere. If she does not do that, the teacher is betraying both the poem and her own artistic sensibility.

At an adult level, the student might consider the particular quality of each image – the choking weeds, the pall of the snow, the insubstantial (and here cold and silent) birds, and so on. Such consideration gives the satisfaction of depth to an appreciation of the poem: it will illuminate the interpretation when read aloud.

The foregoing examples will give some indication of the range of traditional rhymes, though it is a mistake to assign any one exclusively to a particular age group. Whether or not to read a poem aloud to a certain group of children is the decision of the teacher. It is not so much a matter of understanding or not understanding; it is more a matter of taste. Many more poems will be accepted by children who meet them in print. But, generally speaking, as we have said before, the children depend on the teacher to bring alive their taste for poetry of quality.

Branching out from the nursery rhyme are a number of other traditional forms, all of which are useful in their particular ways. The simple horse-riding rhymes learned on mother's knee are extended for older children to include for example, *John Cook Had a Little Grey Mare*, *A Farmer Went Trotting* and *Widdicombe Fair*. Each has its own distinctive rhythm which can be marked (for younger children) by some form of movement. Each has a chorus which enables the class to 'join in' while the teacher speaks the words which tell the story. Many longer ballads and stories such as *King John and the Abbot* and *The Robin Hood Ballads* can be acted or can form part of the background to a historical study of the period. The sea shanties and other work rhymes can be sung or fitted into a historical or geographical context in a similar way.

Students will find it interesting and profitable to trace the influence of nursery rhymes and other traditional verse on the work of modern poets. *The Key of the Kingdom* or other poems in that form seem to have influenced Robert Graves (whether consciously or unconsciously we do not know) in writing his *Warning to Children*, a poem which many teachers will know through the *Oxford Book of Poetry for Children*. Charles Causley has written many original ballads on the traditional pattern, while Ian Serrailier has retold, in a modern idiom, some of the traditional stories and fables. Edith Sitwell's poem, *The King of China's Daughter*, is a delicate transmutation of *I Had a Little Nut Tree*, while *Humpty Dumpty's Poem* (Lewis Carroll) without descending to parody, has many points of contact with *A Man of Words*.

There are endless possibilities for teachers interested in the range and scope of traditional verse to collect and classify verses under various thematic headings – Journeys, Meetings, Dialogues and so on. This would provide something more than a theoretical exercise. It would help to equip the teacher with material for general purposes or to mark a special occasion.

Apart from the influence of the nursery rhyme on children's

language development, Chukovsky makes the point that from the babbling stage onwards young children's language has strong rhythmic and rhyming qualities which make it clearly poetic in origin. He observes, 'In the beginning we are all versifiers. It is only later that we begin to speak in prose'. And this contention is proved convincingly by many examples of children's sayings which are of great interest to the student of language and of poetry.*

* Chukovsky, who died in 1969, is undoubtedly one of the great figures among children's writers and educators. His unique book (now in its twenty-first edition in Russian) *From Two-to-Five* is a study of the linguistic development and thought-forms of pre-school children, and of writing for them. An English translation (by Miriam Morton) was published by the University of California Press in 1968.

3

The Classroom

WE are becoming increasingly convinced that poetry should be moving towards the centre of the curriculum in the primary school, but in the secondary school it is still more commonly treated as being a part of a subject. Here we are not concerned with the teaching of 'Eng.Lit' as part of a specialist study; what we are most certainly concerned with is the position of poetry and the teacher's approach to it. If she is teaching a mixed-ability group in a large comprehensive school or in fact any class in the five to fourteen age range, she should treat poetry as the finest medium of language communication. Of course any teacher of poetry should do this, but here we are not concerned with the examinations' arena and the techniques of survival which characterize so much of the teaching of our older teenagers.

The teacher should aim to expose her pupils to a variety of experiences of the kind that will extend their imaginations, their sense of perspective, their knowledge and their awareness of the power and associations of language. For children language can become a tool or a brush with which to create or fashion; it can be a sound, a sight, a smell or any extension or combination of these; and the child who is imaginatively taught may learn the wonder of self-discovery, of seeing, if you like, into his own heart.

The classroom situation is the background against which we introduce poetry or consider its place in the curriculum, and since it is evident that changes taking place in the schools today are affecting the approach to poetry no less than to any other subject, it is relevant to consider them in a general way. Traditional assumptions are being questioned – about the way in which children learn, about the validity of class structure in schools or streaming, and about the kind of relationship which should exist between children and their teachers.

The momentum for a new outlook on education gathered pace in the infant schools and has spread upwards until it is now being felt in the secondary schools. There it has produced some curricular reform and, particularly interesting to us here, some experiments in integration. The Department of Education and Science (Report no. 40, October 1967) recommended that there should be 'less emphasis on the barriers between traditional subjects and more on their interrelationship', and proposed that 'experience-based learning techniques, developed so successfully in some primary schools, should be used for the humanities at secondary school level'. It is the primary school, therefore, that we take to exemplify the changes of outlook affecting education today.

The classroom in the progressive primary school has been likened to a workshop. The term is appropriate. The very diversity of activity may impress a visitor conditioned to expect a class to be engaged on a single, identifiable 'subject'. Painting, clay-modelling and construction work of various kinds are very much to the fore, but the visitor may not realize that these activities are not now considered as 'frills' or relaxations from the serious business of learning, and they are not separate subjects to be pigeon-holed into separate compartments in the time-table. It is consistent with modern thought to regard a child's activities as part of an experience rather than as practices for one subject or another. In one sense the dramatic play of young children, and the dramatizations of the older ones, are vehicles for communication, as are music making, creative writing or work with tools and materials. Furthermore, they are not isolated from the experience of poetry, which is our concern here; neither are they isolated from intellectual development. They serve the children's needs in many ways, not least as stabilizing agents to the personality, relieving tensions and freeing the spirit for other forms of creative thinking and sensitive response.

There is, in the primary school, an emphasis on *learning* rather than on *teaching*, and this has altered the role of the teacher, stressing the importance of a favourable social climate of learning, rather than a strictly authoritarian regime in which the teacher plays the role of instructor. The emotional development of the children is as much the concern of the modern teacher as is their intellectual development, and in practice it is not possible to separate these two facets. The child's emotional responses, his enthusiasms and drives, his pride in his own skill and achievement, are now the motivating forces whereas, in the past, competition seemed the main incentive to effort. The visitor to the school, therefore, is likely to find evidence of a more child-centred approach to learning. There may well be a more lively, brighter look about even the oldest buildings, with a variety of children's creative writing and painting on the walls, a range of well-illustrated reference books on the shelves, and a comparative absence of the standardized and graded course books which were once calculated to put a straitjacket on normal children's enthusiasm for a subject. The children, too, seem more alive and mobile, and no longer strictly confined within the classroom as they were in the traditional schools. They move about with confidence and act with more initiative and sense of responsibility. If the visitor, bemused in a hive of activity, asks, 'But what lesson is this?', a simple answer may not be possible; and the question, 'What are the children learning?' might be even more difficult. To a perceptive observer the children are obviously learning something, but how is it related to the 'body of knowledge' set down with such authority in the traditional syllabus? We cannot attempt to answer that question here, but it would be fallacious to suggest that the 'body of knowledge' is being by-passed today. In any case, English teaching is concerned to a considerable extent with other criteria, and these conform closely to the values stated by M. V. C. Jefferies in *Personal Values in the Modern World* (Penguin Books). Here he is talking about education as a whole, and not merely of the primary sector :

> Education is the nurture of personal growth. Education as an organized process is concerned not only (or even chiefly) with the knowledge and acquisition of skill, but also with the right attitudes – attitudes towards learning, towards work, towards truth and goodness, towards other people, towards life in general.

It is important as well as characteristic that young children should be eager to explain what they are doing. In school they are encouraged to record everything, at first in speech and later in writing. For the youngest their 'news', what they did or what they found or discovered, is recorded, and from a highly personal point of view, accompanied by personally centred pictures. (But by the time they reach the top of the junior school they will become more skilled in selecting the form of expression suitable to the ideas they wish to express. They will appreciate the need for accuracy in recording, and for imagination in creative writing.) The teacher of young children, particularly, makes capital of whatever is of immediate interest to the child, whether it is a birthday, the weather, or what is happening on the building site. But although the children may show the way, it is still the teacher's responsibility to choose what the children may be doing. The teacher must decide, 'How far shall we go with this? Where is it leading? What is being learned?'

The imaginative teacher instinctively takes the child's viewpoint as her own in organizing much of the activity and exploration which is the substance and the 'method' in educating young children. To depict the atmosphere and the feeling of active learning as she found it in some of the primary schools she visited, Leila Berg coined the phrase 'the wonderful world of the eleven-minus', and we borrow the phrase here to make the point that the child's world is, in a sense, the poet's world also. It is a world of sensory impressions – of sounds, tastes, smells, shapes, movements and colours; a world of personal relationships with things, animals and people; a world of imagination and fantasy. Exploration of this world is the concern of the child and the poet, and poetry in the widest sense is a necessary part of the experience. In fact, although children's language arising spontaneously from their own responses to first-hand experience can be both imaginative and factual, one sometimes finds that their language reflects the fact without the feeling. As children move through the primary school, therefore, they need to develop a sense of the fitness of their language for its particular purpose, and without the experience they will not be able to do this. Modern poetry can offer the richest experience for its qualities of immediacy and personal involvement; for these qualities are attuned to the interests of young children who live almost entirely for the 'here and now' and need to be emotionally involved in what they are learning.

In 'the wonderful world of the eleven-minus' the teacher's function is to select and present experiences in such a way that they make the sharpest possible impact at an emotional level. The experiences may be the children's experiences, but the term 'select' is none the less valid. The word 'present' too is used in its widest sense, and it is true to say that children will often seem to notice and discover what the teacher wants them to look for. There is nothing wrong in this, of course, but the teacher must not be too ready with the word or phrase which seems the most appropriate and obvious, but must rather be sensitive to the tenor of what the child is trying to say. There is a danger of artificiality setting in when the teacher encourages lists of 'good' words to use for descriptive purposes. (No word is a 'good' word in that sense, though literate children are very quick to decorate their writing with words and phrases they think the teacher will approve of.) Sincerity is essential, and though a child may lack the accepted word (which is all too often a cliché in any case), he may do better – he may draw on his own imagination for analogies and metaphors which are poetic in essence. There are, therefore, two tributaries to the main stream – the child's exploration of his own responses to experience and his experience with literature. They both lead to appreciation and to creative writing.

Perhaps we should add here that a poetry *reading* in the classroom is an *occasion*. Unlike many of the activities in the classroom workshop, reading to the class does not lend itself to group work. The teacher therefore has to find the occasion and prepare the children for listening; before she begins, everyone must be 'ready'. The first words of introduction to the reading should have a final quietening effect before the poem is read, and these words should be chosen with as much care as the teacher devotes to the reading itself. With young children, a rearranging of places in order to make a semi-circle – as for listening to a 'story' – is often desirable. Much of this is obvious, but it bears reiteration since interest must be stimulated and held through the personality of the teacher. Needless to say, all the children should be facing the reader.

4

Poetry and Activity

In the primary schools it is established practice for the arts to contribute in a large measure to the breakdown of the traditional subject barriers, and in secondary schools the practice is gaining favour in spite of administrative difficulties with a specialized timetable. The approach is essentially, though not necessarily, on the scale of a project. Poetry can play an important role here, and without disregarding its separate identity the teacher may wish at times to consider a poem in association with other arts, or as a single facet of a total experience. Whether this association is valid or not will depend on whether, for the children, the appreciation of the poem is enhanced in the process. There are many starting points, but here we begin with the poetry and consider whether its particular nature lends itself to association with children's other activities.

In the Shakespearean extracts quoted below, the sensitive adult will feel that although the first appeal may be to the ear, other senses – of movement, sight, touch or smell – may be evoked as part of the whole experience of the reading. In relation to the children at primary school level, the pieces may provide points of reference in a variety of contexts. For example, the general theme of 'Spells' or 'Magic' may be adopted by the class for exploration through the various arts, through history or through creative writing:

> Be not afeard; the isle is full of noises,
> Sounds, and sweet airs, that give delight and hurt not.
> Sometimes a thousand twangling instruments
> Will hum about mine ears; and sometimes voices
> That, if I then had waked after a long sleep,
> Will make me sleep again; and then, in dreaming,
> The clouds methought would open, and show riches

Ready to drop upon me, that when I waked
I cried to dream again.

(*The Tempest*, Act III, Scene 2)

Or, as a contrast:

Round about the cauldron go;
In the poison'd entrails throw. –
  Toad, that under coldest stone,
  Days and nights hath thirty-one
  Swelter'd venom sleeping got,
  Boil thou first i' the charmed pot!

  Double, double toil and trouble;
  Fire, burn; and cauldron bubble.

Fillet of a fenny snake,
In the cauldron boil and bake.
Eye of newt and toe of frog,
Wool of bat and tongue of dog,
Adder's fork and blind worm's sting,
Lizard's leg and owlet's wing,
For a charm of powerful trouble,
Like a hell-broth boil and bubble.

  Double, double toil and trouble;
  Fire, burn; and cauldron, bubble.

(*Macbeth*, Act IV, Scene 1)

In a drama lesson, associated scenes at the children's level may be improvised and the emotional content of the poetry expressed through movement. This is not, of course, 'acting Shakespeare'. But, through 'Waking up on an enchanted island', or 'Being a wizard making magic spells', the child is deepening his capacity to appreciate the magic of Shakespeare's words. On the other hand, in the next example the children are interpreting Shakespeare's words, though not in the terms of the play:

You spotted snakes with double tongue,
  Thorny hedgehogs, be not seen.
Newts and blindworms, do no wrong,
Come not near our fairy queen.

> *Philomel with melody*
> *Sing in our sweet lullaby,*
> *Lulla, lulla, lullaby; lulla, lulla, lullaby.*
>   *Never harm*
>   *Nor spell nor charm*
> *Come our lovely lady nigh.*
> *So good night, with lullaby.*

> *Weaving spiders, come not here;*
>   *Hence, you longlegged spinners, hence!*
> *Beetles black, approach not near,*
>   *Worm nor snail, do no offence.*

> *Philomel with melody*
> *Sing in our sweet lullaby,*
> *Lulla, lulla, lullaby; lulla, lulla, lullaby.*
>   *Never harm*
>   *Nor spell nor charm*
> *Come our lovely lady nigh.*
> *So goodnight, with lullaby.*

> *Hence, away! Now all is well.*
> *One aloof stand sentinel!*
>   (*A Midsummer Night's Dream*, Act II, Scene 2)

After the first reading, the children will be invited to interpret the movement of each of the creatures in turn. The sound and rhythm of each line must be distinctive enough to convey quite clearly the character of the movement. This may be discussed if the teacher thinks it necessary, but the key will be in the reading. The lines will be delivered vigorously as if to actively banish possibly unwilling creatures from the presence of the queen. The children will select a dominating feature for emphasis in each line – the hissing sibilants and the 'double-tongue' give the clue for the snakes; the spiky, changeable shape of the hedgehog; the slimy, slithery quality of the newts and blindworms; the thin, scampering movement of the spiders; the hard solidity of the beetles. These characteristics will be most effectively suggested by lightness and flexibility in the teacher's voice.

By contrast, the chorus, 'Philomel with melody...' is lyrical. It calls for graceful, undulating movement. On the other hand, it may be felt that it is desirable to change the movement at 'Never harm ...', which may be regarded as the climax of the incantation in which the spell is wound up. The movement may be worked out on this individual basis, all children taking each part in turn; and it may well be left there. But, if desired, parts could be given and the whole arranged as a group scene.

Though these extracts from Shakespeare may strike chords in the children's own fantasies, often a reference point may be found in the context of their everyday experience. In *Boy Fishing*, which we quote on page 46, an interest in this sport would hardly add to the appeal or to the appreciation, and it seems irrelevant to include it merely because the children may be 'doing a topic' on the subject. A more valid point of reference is the feeling of contentment which has come to us all, at times, when we are entirely involved in something we are doing – the pleasure which may come when we are *alone*, but not *lonely*. This thought is, for example, expressed in Wordsworth's much-quoted *Daffodils*, a poem which frequently appears in anthologies for children. But there the concept is adult, and the experience of responding emotionally to a field of wild flowers is one which is very remote, we feel, from children. In whatever terms the teacher may explain it, the poem cannot really appeal through the children's own experience or through their imaginations. There may be other reasons for including it, of course, but if so the teacher should consider them rather than assume that it is a good poem for children because it is by a major poet and included in children's anthologies. What can the children make of:

> For oft, when on my couch I lie
>   In vacant or in pensive mood,
> They flash upon that inward eye
>   Which is the bliss of solitude;
> And then my heart with pleasure fills,
>   And dances with the daffodils.

By contrast, in *Boy Fishing* (E. V. Scovell) the theme is not stated directly, but it is implicit and readily understood. Furthermore, as in many of the best poems, discussion reveals new depths of meaning, even to the adult.

BOY FISHING

I am cold and alone,
On my tree-root sitting as still as stone.
The fish come to my net. I scorned the sun,
The voices on the road, and they have gone.
My eyes are buried in the cold pond, under
The cold, spread leaves; my thoughts are silver-wet.
I have ten stickleback, a half-day's plunder,
Safe in my jar. I shall have ten more yet.

The following points may, or may not, emerge as the result of discussion. They will certainly not come in order, nor as a result of the first reading. Some may become talking points for future readings, if the class like the poem and would enjoy hearing it again; but though the teacher may hope that it would be an acceptable addition to the class's store of poetry, this cannot be pre-determined.

The overall feeling of the poem is one of omnipotence or of magic power. (Is this feeling characteristic of other forms of 'chase' or does it apply particularly to fishing?) As I sit 'as still as stone' (the image is appropriate to the environment), 'the fish *come* to my net. I *scorned* the sun'. The images convey the god-like attitude of the fisherman. The words 'plunder', 'spread', 'silver-wet', 'cold' are charged with additional meaning from the context in which they are used. Notice how the details of the environment, including the time of day, are significantly employed to establish the mood of the poem; and notice the satisfying, if almost prosaic, statement in the last two lines.

A follow-up of the poem is not strictly necessary, but the teacher may, preferably at another time, ask children to choose a situation of solitude and concentration, say 'Alone on the seashore making a sandcastle', and tell them to write about this in a poem.

A point of view is an aspect of relationship, and as such is a subject of fundamental concern and growing complexity throughout our lives. Some relationships can, of course, be measured mathematically, while others are relationships of feeling, but in one sense there is no essential distinction between the two. They are both facets of total experience. With children, the affective element naturally comes first, and leads to the desire to measure, just as at a certain stage an appreciation of scale values may grow out of an interest in car models or dolls' furniture. The poet's primary concern is with the emotional element in relationships, and he pursues this theme in a variety of ways. Let us take a simple example:

SLOWLY · James Reeves

Slowly the tide creeps up the sand,
Slowly the shadows cross the land.
Slowly the cart-horse pulls his mile,
Slowly the old man mounts the stile.

Slowly the hands move round the clock,
Slowly the dew dries on the dock.
Slow is the snail – but slowest of all
The green moss spreads on the old brick wall.

The poem draws on traditional images of myth or more humble folklore – the sand, tide and shadows on the one hand, and the carthorse and stile on the other. Through the medium of these images it explores various aspects of time – the rhythms or regular patterns of the days and seasons, the continuous, steady effort of the cart-horse or, with the old man, the sense of approaching death and the possibility of new life on the other side of the 'stile'. Finally, the snail and the green moss are further aspects of rhythm and change. The children can 'understand' the poem with their feelings, though not in the terms that we have used. Perhaps they might write their own 'Slowly' or 'Quickly' poems.

Experiences in looking with attention can be used in a context of activity within the classroom and near environment of the school. Various viewpoints can be adopted, such as looking from below, looking down from a height, looking through a magnifying-glass or into a distorting mirror, moving the source of light and so on. Such experiences, when discussed or otherwise reinforced, can help to develop poetic insight, if one may use the term to indicate an ability to see with new eyes, or to 'find new worlds within the known world'. The poet often helps to make such experiences articulate for the children. Take, for instance, the following short poem:

THE EAGLE · Tennyson

He clasps the crag with crooked hands;
Close to the sun in lonely lands,
Ring'd with the azure world he stands.

The wrinkled sea beneath him crawls;
He watches from his mountain walls,
And like a thunderbolt he falls.

Here, in every line there is a different feeling, partly dependent on the constantly changing viewpoint. We are identified with the eagle as the poet directs us to look up, then around in an arc (Ring'd with the azure world'), and finally, down. The watchful stillness of the bird of prey (which is evident to all who have visited a zoo) is depicted not only by the suddenness of the fall, but also through the aerial images which precede it.

The quality of identification is a characteristic of modern poetry dealing with animals. Animals are regarded with compassion but generally without the cloying sentiment which so often marred children's poetry of an earlier age. We chose the following example because to find a dead bird is within the experience of most children whether they live in town or country; moreover, the viewpoint is an adult one with which the children can readily identify their own feelings:

BLACKBIRD · Christopher Leach

My wife saw it first –
I was reading the evening paper.
Come and look, she said.

It was trying to drink
Where water had formed on a drain-cover.
It was shabby with dying.
It did not move until I was very close –
Then hopped off, heavily,
Disturbing dead leaves.

We left water, crumbs.
It did not touch them
But waited among the leaves,
Silently.

This morning was beautiful:
Sunlight, other birds
Singing.

It was outside the door.
I picked it up
And it was like holding feathered air.
I wrapped what was left
Incongruously
In green sycamore leaves
And buried it near the tree
Inches down.

This evening
I find it difficult to concentrate
On the paper, the news
Of another cosmonaut.

The teacher will value such examples as this which help to show children that poetry does not *always* depend on a strict pattern of rhyme and metre. Apart from the quality of the writing, this freedom of form is one of the contributions that modern poetry can make to the children's own creative writing. In reading *Blackbird* the teacher will notice how the form chosen fits the viewpoint taken. A closer sense of involvement may be achieved, and the pathos of the situation heightened rather than diminished by the natural rhythm of speech used by the poet. The keynote of the poem is perhaps struck by the use of the word 'incongruously', and here the teacher will probably need to find a synonym – perhaps 'out of place'. In different ways the incongruity is shown by the beautiful weather, with other birds singing; by the behaviour of the sick bird, and the careful burial; and the 'news of another cosmonaut'. These points may emerge without 'telling' the children, if the right questions are asked. The poem could be placed in a context of classroom experience including direct observation by the children

D

of birds living in close proximity to human beings; or perhaps in the wider context of 'Our responsibility for our pets'.

The next example appeals to the children's inner life of fantasy. As a topic, one or other of the *Elements* is full of opportunities for creative work in art, music, movement, writing or drama, and there are many poems suitable for children on this theme:

THE SEA · James Reeves

The sea is a hungry dog,
Giant and grey.
He rolls on the beach all day.
With his clashing teeth and shaggy jaws
Hour upon hour he gnaws
The rumbling, tumbling stones,
And 'Bones, bones, bones, bones!'
The giant sea-dog moans,
Licking his greasy paws.

And when the night wind roars
And the moon rocks in the stormy cloud,
He bounds to his feet and snuffs and sniffs,
Shaking his wet sides over the cliffs,
And howls and hollos long and loud.

But on quiet days in May or June,
When even the grasses on the dune
Play no more their reedy tune,
With his head between his paws
He lies on the sandy shores,
*   So quiet, so quiet, he scarcely snores.*

The poem makes a strong emotional appeal to most children even on its first hearing. But subsequent readings and discussion reveal the close unity of the sound picture of the 'hungry dog'. Images evoking the sound of the rough sea (moans and bones, for example) are balanced by others ('Shaking his wet sides over the cliffs') which have a stronger visual appeal. But often the poem's aural and visual qualities are fused into a single image – 'With his clashing teeth and shaggy jaws', and 'rumbling, tumbling stones'; and the sense of taste is involved too, in the phrase 'licking his greasy paws'. The children will enjoy the poem through the way the reader relishes the sounds. There must be no holding back in the reading here but, in contrast, the last verse can be taken as quietly as possible.

Poets often use some degree of personification in their poems about the elements, and this is the way that children write about them. Many of the stories from ancient mythology contribute to the children's feeling for the power and mystery of the elements. Obviously there are many other areas of exploration in addition to the elements, and the activities that we have suggested are essentially associated with poetry rather than an integral part of it; the most *direct* activity for children is poetry speaking, and choral speaking is its most handy form for classroom purposes. Some years ago when it was more widely practised, choral speaking developed almost into an art form in some schools, but as such it has largely died out partly because an element of direction and repetitive practice is necessary to 'polish' the speaking, and partly because other values in poetry are now predominating.

Apart from some of the folk rhymes mentioned in Chapter 2, most poetry does not make its impact so well when spoken chorally, indeed it can easily be spoilt. However, there is no shortage of material for the teacher who wishes to experiment (see Appendix). The decision really rests on how far one should go with an activity which requires techniques, or seeks to develop them – techniques of voice production, listening and timing both on an individual and on a group level. The analogy with the school or class 'choir' is obvious, but most teachers would regard singing as a more essential activity. However, many teachers have found that choral speaking is worth while as long as it remains within the capacity of the children who need to achieve a quick and satisfying result. It is an activity which should supplement, rather than be a substitute for, the individual appreciation of poetry which children develop through reading poetry for themselves and through the medium of the teacher's voice.

The poems most suitable for choral speaking in the junior school are usually the shanties, ballads and narrative poems of the traditional type. But there are others which have a group situation built into their structure. Essentially, they are extrovert rather than contemplative in their appeal. *The Fair*, by David Shavreen, is particu-

larly suitable for choral treatment. It is not beginner's material, and
it needs practice, but it should not prove too difficult to raise the
speaking to a standard which does no disservice to the poem and
maintains the level of enjoyment throughout. The arrangement for
voices is the poet's:

THE FAIR

All the   *Music tinkles and jangles and shrills,*
class   *The air is loud with the blare of the fair,*
          The clamour of voices fills all the hollow,
          All the town is there.

Group 1   *From the top of the hill it's a magic city*
          Teeming with life like an eastern bazaar.
Group 2   *The minaret of the helter-skelter,*
          Summons the children near and far;
Group 3   *A huge wheel turns as though it were grinding*
          Invisible grain for a giant's bread,
          Bearing its cargo of laughing people
          High in the sky overhead:
All the   *And stretching streets of tented stalls*
class   *Echo with the familiar calls.*

Boy-solo *Three shots for sixpence,*
          Knock 'em down,
          They're lovely and milky
          Hairy and brown!
          Half way for women
          And children too.
          Have a go sweetheart
          I'll give one to you.

All the   *The spluttering pipes of the merry-go-round*
girls   *Welcome the throng with a wheezy sound,*
          Playing old tunes as the steeds leave the ground.
All   *'Merrily we roll along, roll along, roll along,*
          Merrily we roll along', goes the incessant song.

Girl-solo   *How strong are you?*
                 Here's a bag to punch
                 And a bell to strike
                 And a bar to crunch.
                 Show you're a man
                 Like Hercules
                 And you'll carry off
                 A prize, with ease.

G. 1   *We ride to the moon on a pathway of cloud,*
and 2   *We champ at our bits when the music grows loud,*
                 'Merrily we race along o'er the dark blue sea'.

G. 1   *Sit at the wheel of your Dodgem car,*
                 Testing your hand and your eagle eye,
                 Pitting your wits and your nerveless skill
                 Against the bullies of the track
                 In hot pursuit.
G. 2   *Your mouth feels dry,*
                 There's no escape, they're at your back.
All   *A twist of the wheel and a squeeze of your foot*
                 You've dodged past the danger
                 And come to a halt.

G. 2   *We sail by the stars and our nostrils quiver*
and 3   *As we plunge in the waters of the Milky River.*
                 Merrily we ride along, ride along for ever.

Girls in G. 1   *Time for refreshment.*
Girls in G. 2   *A bottle of pop,*
Boys in G. 1   *An ice-cream cornet*
                 Full to the top,
Boys in G. 2   *A candy floss*
                 Whisked into thread
Girls in G. 3   *Silky and sweet*
                 With crystals of red,

G. 1   *Back past the plants Uranus and Neptune*
                 We gallop to earth and we'll be there soon.

Solo voice 1	*I've won a dolly on the Housey-Housey.*
Solo voice 2	*Did you see the giant rat?*
Solo voice 3	*I looked funny in the Hall of Mirrors.*
Solo voice 4	*Wasn't the Fat Lady fat?*
Solo voice 5	*I had a go at shooting with a pistol*
	But I couldn't knock the last cat flat.
Solo voice 6	*Look at Bertie, it says Kiss Me*
	All round the brim of his sailor's hat.
G. 2	*Round and round and round and round,*
	Our journey's over, we've reached the ground.
All	*Farewell children,*
	We're bound
	To leave you
	Now.

This serves to indicate another area, we feel, which can be explored by those interested in developing the resources of poetry; and, as we shall see in the following chapters, the knowledge of those resources may give rise to what is, in our opinion, one of the most positive and exciting results, the practice of creative writing.

5

Material and Experience

As we have suggested, the quality of a poetic experience in the classroom does not have a direct relationship to the quality of the material we use. Poetry of lesser quality may be best fitted for certain purposes, as with verse for choral speaking, poetry for direct translation into dramatic terms and poetry for musical or sound-making accompaniment. On the other hand, the essence of poetic experience is in listening and in contemplating, and here the quality of the material would seem to be of overriding importance. Even so, the total experience can only be evaluated in terms of the practical situation, affected as it is by the delicate balance of personal relationships between the class and the teacher.

At all times the teacher is aware of the necessity to use her own personality or personal qualities to influence the climate of the classroom, and the nature of poetry and its flexibility in use is such that it can always be 'there' as her ally. The habit of using poetry incidentally is one for which the teacher needs to prepare herself by having a variety of poems handy to suit the occasion. Opportunities for a poem (perhaps a brief verse spoken by the children, perhaps one read to them) will occur often during a normal day, and the sensitive teacher will know when it is psychologically 'right' to take advantage of the opportunity.

In some cases a poem may by its impact create its own change in the atmosphere; or perhaps a particular choice may be suggested by some delicate affinity for a mood which has already been established; or perhaps, less subtly, the subject of the poem may be fitting to the occasion. Young children are particularly susceptible to fortuitous events which affect the atmosphere in the classroom (the weather is an obvious example), and since the teacher cannot hope to ignore these changes altogether, she may seek to meet them or better still to use them beneficially.

The material for this incidental use of poetry need by no means be confined to the school anthologies or to complete poems. The teacher's own personal reading of adult poetry will provide quotable extracts as will her knowledge of the 'classics' which, however unsuitable in their entirety, can provide illuminating experiences in many contexts. Shelley's picture of autumn leaves as 'like ghosts from an enchanter fleeing' or as 'pestilence stricken multitudes' are two of the many examples which the teacher might wish to introduce into the junior school long before the whole poem could have any significance.

Above all, the experience of poetry follows a cyclical rather than a linear pattern of growth, and that is why sets of poetry books are extremely limited and generally unsuitable for the purpose for which they were intended. We learn and we re-learn, sometimes from the same material and sometimes from a variety of sources which reveal different aspects of the same truth. In so far as poetry is concerned with subjects or concepts, these are best considered as areas of experience to which the child and the adult continually return in order to deepen their understanding. The following quotations might be compared in more than one sense:

1 *Twinkle, twinkle, little star,*
   How I wonder what you are,
   Up above the world so high,
   Like a diamond in the sky.

2 *Twinkle, twinkle, little bat,*
   How I wonder what you're at;
   Up above the world so high,
   Like a tea-tray in the sky.

3 *Tiger, tiger, burning bright*
   In the forests of the night,
   What immortal hand or eye,
   Could frame thy fearful symmetry?

The relationship between 1 and 2 is obvious, and we might generalize to the extent of saying that Carroll's parody comes best when a child outgrows the superficial or two-dimensional quality of the first poem. But the relationship of the nursery rhyme with

Blake's *Tiger* is not so simple, nor can we assess the suitability of each so precisely to children of a particular age group.

Both poems are comparable in some ways. They are almost identical in rhythm and rhyming pattern, and in a sense they are both aspects of the same theme – wonder at the infinite. But to accept one for children and reject the other would reflect a superficial judgment. On what criteria would we base our choice? We are certain that one is a more adult poem than the other, and we *might* agree that one is more worthwhile for children; but it is obvious that we are now moving on to dangerous ground. From experience we know that Blake's poem is one to live with in increasing depth from the early days of school through to adulthood; the other becomes less and less significant as we get older. There is place for both, and children will tend to grow out of the nursery verse stage as they come to prefer pieces like Carroll's parody.

Choice of material is as much a matter of balance as of acceptance or rejection of an individual poem. Most of the favourites of an earlier generation are still acceptable in schools today (and they still appear in anthologies). But in so far as adult's and children's ways of life and sets of values are not the same as they were before the Second World War, this will be reflected in our choice of poetry. A new outlook is particularly needed in the transition between the primary and the secondary school.

The teaching of poetry, like the teaching of other subjects, is affected by the arbitrary division in English education which is still made at eleven-plus, but in most cases the affects on teaching methods are far greater than they need be. The experience of poetry should not be completely isolated from that of other arts, and in spite of the fact that the child is delivered at eleven-plus from the one familiar pair of hands to the specialized attention of seven or eight individuals, experiments in subject integration have been successfully carried out in many secondary schools. We have stressed the need for poetry to move towards the centre of the curriculum in the earlier stages of a child's education, and we feel that it should continue to act as a positive link between subjects and activities in the late primary and early secondary stages. Its place in language development remains paramount.

The child at eleven or thereabouts moves from the general to the specific, from the integrated to the seemingly disparate. It is therefore vital that as he makes contact with the formulae of mathematics, the rudiments of science in this age of technology, and as perhaps he accepts the challenge of a foreign language, he is made strongly aware of the abiding challenge of his own language. In the final year of the primary school in fact many children will be undertaking work of the nature mentioned above, and in the first years of the secondary school all but the most backward will be doing what is commonly called academic work, however limited their direction or achievement. It will be seen, therefore, that it is vital for the teacher of poetry, regardless of the ability of her children, to make sure that the manifold experiences of her own language are available for discussion, interpretation and perhaps extension in terms of activity. As we said earlier, there will be a time to go deeply into an experience and a time to just read and listen; a time to evaluate the spiritual or moral or practical views uttered, and a time to accept or contemplate the essential beauty or distillation involved.

The choice of poetry to be presented to children is, as always, most important, and should be the result of the teacher's own explorations, and not just drawn from any anthology which is allocated to the class. It is true, however, that compilers of anthologies are often careful not to be precise as to the ages of the children for whom the poetry is intended. This is a wise precaution. So much depends on a number of factors, but most particularly on the enthusiasm and skill of the reader, a point which we have made earlier but which we must once again stress.

Material for use at upper junior/lower secondary level will, in some instances, be indistinguishable from that introduced earlier in terms of basic content, for it will include traditional verse of the kind widely used with younger children – the Robin Hood ballads, sea shanties, the Pied Piper, John Gilpin and other narrative poems, all too well-known to need commentary here. They will always hold their place on intrinsic appeal, and they are now found additionally helpful as starting points for projects (particularly those with an historical bias, as well as for drama, choral speaking and music). There is no need to replace this much-used material, but every opportunity should be taken to add to it.

There is always a place for light verse, and the mildly satirical verse of poets like Thomas Hood and Hilaire Belloc and others will no doubt continue to be used. Again, some poets of our own time have added to the available material. James Reeves's *Prefabulous*

Animiles and Ted Hughes's *Meet My Folks* are two of the better-known collections which could be added to T. S. Eliot's *Old Possum's Book of Practical Cats*. The 'silly' verses of Spike Milligan, or the more sophisticated work of Ogden Nash, may appeal to some. A wide variety of material should be sampled, but although our own emphasis would be firmly on the appeal of contemporary verse, there is every reason to explore the established English poets with discrimination and the critical eye of selection. One thinks, for instance, of Blake :

THE CHIMNEY SWEEPER

A little black thing among the snow,
Crying 'Weep! Weep!' in notes of woe!
Where are thy father and mother, say?'—
'They are both gone up to the church to pray.

'Because I was happy upon the heath,
And smiled among the winter's snow,
They clothed me in the clothes of death,
And taught me to sing the notes of woe.

'And because I am happy and dance and sing,
They think they have done me no injury,
And are gone to praise God and His Priest and King,
Who make up a heaven of our misery.'

Teachers and children alike may find this a challenging poem, but it is so imbued with compassion and social and moral comment that it could provide material for discussion of the problems of poverty and deprivation in Blake's time and our own. Obviously the teacher will need to tell the class about the iniquitous employment of child chimney-sweepers in Blake's time and in the early Victorian period. The possibilities of discussion and project work are self-evident, and need not be explored here.

Clare, too, is another poet who repays investigation, as we saw from *Clock-a-clay* in Chapter 2. Again the historical context of his work, the condition of the rustic poor, the parallels with our own day can all be explored, as well as the central aspects – his seeing nature minutely, imaginatively, with his eye close to the object, qualities which may make us and our children look again with a seeing, feeling eye, at what we pass by so often without attention. In fact we feel that it would be true to say that to read Clare is to focus on the natural beauty which is our inheritance if we can but train our eyes to see it. A teacher may feel that Shelley (*The Cloud* perhaps), Keats (*Meg Merrilies, La Belle Dame Sans Merci*), Wordsworth (*The Solitary Reaper* but *not* the Lucy poems) and Coleridge (*Kubla Khan*) all have something to offer to children. But these – and Tennyson – should not be chosen in order to create an establishment of great poets, they should be used to enlarge historical, social, sensual, spiritual experience and knowledge or purely for the description, speculation, basic enjoyment which children may derive from them.

In our choice of material we should not be guided by reputation but by the quality of the experience offered, the strong stamp of individuality which stimulates the intellect and the imagination in response. We do not intend here to provide a catalogue of 'suitable' poets. The bibliography to this book may be used as a starting point and then the teacher may explore for herself. But we must mention D. H. Lawrence because he was intrumental in bringing about a freer and more enlightened attitude towards the various forms of poetry. Many of his animal poems (*Mountain Lion, Bat* and *Snake*, for instance) foreshadow modern appraisals, and since his novels, stories and poems are likely to appeal to the teacher *at her own level*, he forms an important sympathetic link, so to speak, between teacher and children. And, as we have indicated, we feel that the teacher's emphasis should be on modern verse because of its flexibility, its use of compelling and perhaps unusual contemporary idiom and, most important of all, because it often utters the obsessions, social, spiritual and moral, of its time.

One would hope to find, in any current anthology, a selection of work by contemporary poets. We cannot be overconcerned at this stage with the precocious child who delights in the *Ode to a Nightingale* at the age of thirteen. What we are concerned with is to capture the interest of children of widely divergent ability by exposing them to highly individualistic and positive language. Our aim must be to get them to think, to evaluate (in the non-academic sense of that word) and ultimately to write with a greater degree of satisfaction and, one hopes, insight, than they have hitherto known. As always, and we cannot repeat this enough, the overmastering need is for the teacher to be receptive to the poetic experience. In fact, much of the poetry which she will teach will not have been written specifically for children; it will be adult in conception and execution, and the teacher should aim at a comprehensive appraisal of each poem she teaches *before* she begins to teach it. Let us take, for example, a poem by Norman MacCaig which seems suitable for reading and discussion by the twelve- to thirteen-year-old age group :

GRANTON

A shunting engine butts them
And the long line of wagons
   Abruptly pours out
Iron drops from a bottle.

A flare fizzes, discovers
Tarry sheds, a slipway
Tasselled with weeds
And a boat with oars akimbo.

On the oily skin of the water
And coils and whorls, all oily,
   Of green and blue;
They sparkle with filthy coal dust.

Night crouches beyond the harbour,
Powerful, black as a panther
   That suddenly.
Opens a yellow eye.

Note that the poem consists of subtle variations of movement, stillness and colour. The images are concise and immediately influence the reader's response. The shunting engine is invested with animal images which at first sight are unconnected with the menace that characterizes the panther image in the last verse. Yet there is an implication in this transition of the essential difference between the known and the unknown, between what man has made in the model of an animal – the engine – and what is primitive and fearful in the animal kingdom, the killer or panther of the jungle, night. Immediately certain associations have been set up by the poet and, better still, the pictures created and the sound of the words all combine to achieve a composite effect, the kind of effect which is seen in a fine painting, or heard in a piece of music.

It is not suggested that the class as a whole will recognize this, although with the aid of the teacher they should come to some positive appraisal. For example, the sounds of the vowels and the consonants in their different patterns might be looked at. What makes 'A flare fizzes' immediately effective within the atmosphere of the poem? On the other hand, what does the phrase 'Iron drops from a bottle' contribute to that atmosphere and to our appreciation of the scene? With what would you usually associate the word 'akimbo' and why do you think the poet has chosen to use it here? What does the poet's use of the word 'sparkle' when he is describing the 'filthy coal dust' tell us about his attitude? Another interesting aspect of the poem is that it contains no rhyme, yet it has a set form which demands a certain number of syllables to the line and an equal number of lines to the verse. In what way does this technical regularity reflect the nature of the poem? Doubtless any discussion with an intelligent and imaginative group will cover more than this, but with a less able group the teacher will have to contribute correspondingly more to the analysis herself.

The imaginative teacher who sees clearly that poetry can be used as a bridge between the subjects will perhaps wish to explore the possibilities of project work and creative writing arising from poetry such as this. For example, geographical or historical projects on railways, harbours, or on Granton itself and its particular importance could be undertaken either individually or in groups. Ideally, there will be cooperation from other subject teachers, but always there are books to be had from the school and public libraries which will assist individual research. The project need not be an extended one; a report back by the groups on what they have discovered may add much to the general and specific knowledge of the class as a whole. It may, indeed, spark off ideas and interests in the individual which will provide meaningful and rewarding experiences in later life. Yet in a sense this is giving to poetry a utilitarian, functional limitation which is far from being elevated or inspired; poetry can be exciting or rich in terms of experience, or it can communicate, or merely state, a vision, an attitude, or paint a picture which requires no commentary, invites no elaboration and which would hardly stand any extension. Obviously the teacher, through her own reading and judgment, must decide when to merely read, when to promote discussion and when to extend into activity and further experience. We would suggest that the class should be given time to think freely about poetry which they have just had read to them or which they have read themselves. They will often make suggestions for research and writing which the teacher had not considered. For such is the unique appeal of poetry that it is all things to all men, and therefore something different to each of us.

The appeal of most modern poetry depends largely on the sympathetic chord it strikes in the individual reader. What is readily seen and imaginatively felt by one person is either incomprehensible or dull to another, and a major part of the teaching of poetry is concerned with exploring the variety of interpretations, responses and opinions, however subjective, which the reading of a single poem evokes. Thus the greater the teacher's range, the greater the variety of experiences presented to the children and the greater their own imaginative development. We must stress and stress again that there is no place for the narrowly academic approach which is concerned merely with comprehension. To teach a poem is to live it, and to read it with that attention to meaning, suggestion and associations which makes it live for those who are listening. Once heard, it will never again be thought of as dead words on a page.

Fortunately, today, there are many good anthologies in existence which encourage teachers to break the fetters of inflexible teaching. Even if it is not possible for each child in the class to have his own copy, the teacher is free to use material from such books as *Here Today* (ed. Ted Hughes, Hutchinson), *Every Man Will Shout* (ed. R. Mansfield and I. Armstrong, Oxford University Press), the three volumes of *Voices* (ed. Geoffrey Summerfield, Penguin Books) and *Happenings* (ed. M. Wollman and D. Grugeon, Harrap). Do not be deterred by the fact that, for example, *The Albemarle Book of Modern Verse* (ed. F. E. S. Finn, John Murray) and *Rhyme and Reason* (ed. R. O'Malley and D. Thompson, Chatto & Windus) have become set books, for their range of modern verse, as with *This Day and Age* (ed. S. Hewett, Arnold) is a wide and stimulating one. In *Rhyme and Reason*, for example, the poems are grouped under headings ('Town Life', 'War', Machinery', etc.). The interested student or teacher may in turn be moved to make her own headings, perhaps for a class anthology. One may even find that the class will sort out the headings they want, and complete their own individual and group anthologies. This could, of course, in turn lead to projects or assignments in history, or any meaningful ventures arising from a cluster of related poems. There is always the possibility, though it need not be strained too far, of reading poems which invite contrast with one another.

There is, for example, a poem by Sylvia Plath called *Mushrooms*, with a superbly menacing opening:

> *Overnight, very*
> *Whitely, discreetly,*
> *Very quietly,*
> *Our toes, our noses,*
> *Take hold on the loam,*
> *Acquire the air.*

This can be contrasted in terms of mood, overtones and technique with Boris Pasternak's *Picking Mushrooms*, which begins:

> *Roads and milestones.*
> *Trees and ditches.*
> *We shuffle away*
> *To look for mushrooms,*
> *One by one*
> *Dive out of daylight . . .*

The teacher's aim should be to stimulate and extend, to provide the basis for experience and the imaginative participation in what is unknown, untasted and unfelt until the language of poetry gives it life.

6

Creative Writing

No book on teaching poetry can ignore children's own writing; it is very much in the stream of general teaching as well as germane to an appreciation of poetry. Creative writing as we know it is a modern development and the product of a new outlook. Many traditional schools which obtain high standards from their pupils in some of the more formal aspects of education have not yet produced writing of any quality throughout the school. This may be because such writing cannot essentially be 'taught' (though, like a taste for poetry, it can be 'caught'); or it may be because in the more formal schools poetry itself is undervalued.

Our purpose in including examples of children's writing here is not primarily to show how similar work can be produced in other schools (that would be somewhat presumptuous), nor is it only to show the standard that can be reached, though indeed that is a small part of our purpose. Chiefly we hope to demonstrate that children's own creative writing can make a contribution to a teacher's own appreciation of poetry in general. The gap between modern poetry and children's writing has narrowed significantly to such an extent that they can, for the first time we think, be seen as tributaries of the same stream. Thus the brief analysis or commentary which we make on the children's poems is not only directed to our function as teachers, but rather to our own personal capacity to enjoy poetry.

The free writing of infants is usually in prose, but the distinction is one of content rather than of form. Very young children like to write a 'story', and it is the development of the plot which determines the narrative form of their writing. Within the compass of the story we may find some poetic expression (if we may use the term without overtones of affectation or precocity), but the young

E

child is most concerned to move from one incident to the next without pausing to probe deeply in any part of the sequence.

As an occasional alternative to the free writing of a story, young children may be invited to concentrate on the particular impact of an experience, whether imaginary or contrived. We suggest this tentatively because too much structuring of the experience would be wrong at this stage. The important aspect is the flow, or what has sometimes been called 'talking with the pen'. Nevertheless, even the yougest children can use poetic imagery to express some depth of feeling and perception, as in the following example from a child in an infant school:

> Boom, go the fireworks
> Like battles in the sky
> until they die
> upon the black sky

With young children the linear divisions may be an intuitive way of meeting the need for punctuation, or for expressing rhythm and emphasis – sometimes children underline or use capitals to make their meaning clearer and to suggest how their poems should sound. On the other hand, we should not seek to read significance into the line structure where probably none exists. Speculation is interesting when it is exercised by a sensitive teacher who knows the child or at least knows children. In the case of the poems we quote from the youngest age range we do not know whether the children wrote them in the literal sense, or spoke them to a sympathetic adult who wrote down what she understood the child to say. That hardly matters if the result seems true to the nature of the child. We find these examples unaffected and charming, and suitable for our purpose here in revealing to a sensitive adult the well-springs of poetic expression which may lie dormant or pass unnoticed by some teachers. In the junior school the danger of failing to recognize true quality when one meets it is even more apparent.

The poems that we quote immediately below were written for the Brooke Bond's Children's Writing Competition. No distinction was made in the schedule between poetry and prose writing, and this seems wise. We call them 'poems' to distinguish them from 'stories', and it seems that the experience of imaginative listening was successful here in giving the very young primary school children a wide range of personal choice with an unlimited opportunity for digressing. On the other hand, attention was focussed for them on their *feelings* in relation to the experience:

> *I stood in the garden,*
> *as quiet as can be,*
> *and do you know what*
> *I heard,*
> *I heard a bumble bee.*
> *It went buzz-buzz-buzz.*
> *I walked down the lane*
> *today*
> *and heard a reservoir a big*
> *big reservoir in the distance.*
> *I walked right into the wood*
> *as well*
> *and do you know I heard a*
> *church bell ring,*
> *I walked and heard a faint*
> *faint blast of a quarry.*
> *I heard a bird sing a song*
> *of spring.*
> *I heard my mother calling its time*
> *for dinner.*
> *So I sadly had to walk back from*
> *the woods*
> *past the quarry and down the lane*
> *until I came and stood in my*
> *own garden*
> *as quiet as quiet can be.*

> Diane Martin (Calver, Derbyshire)

In general one becomes aware of the child's instinctive feeling for distance in relation to herself, her power of recalling things out of sight by means of their sound and, above all, the sense of 'form' in the journey, beginning and ending in the garden. In the next poem, by contrast, there is a concentration almost to the point of inaction, as the malevolent sound attacks the child. The 'happy' interlude makes a pleasant contrast:

> When I am alone
> I hear a high-pitched
> sound. It feels like two
> pencils being put in
> my ears. When I am
> happy I hear bells
> and a band playing.
> Sometimes I hear a fizzing
> sound and I feel my
> head going fizzee.
> When I am doing a sum
> and I know what it is
> but I cannot think of it
> it feels like a bit of
> my brain has fallen
> down to my body
> and rockets are firing
> into my head.

Richard Grey (Fife)

The writer of the next poem identifies himself with the wind in his wish for power. The unconventional capitals may indicate the importance to the poem of these key words:

> I would like to be the
> Wind because I could
> make fires get bigger
> and I could blow people's
> hats off. I could squirt
> water in people's faces.
> And I could make the
> Sea rough and Sink
> Ships and Boats.
> If I feel in a good mood I would
> dry mummy's washing.

Gerald Berkley (Lancing, Sussex)

The next poem sees the Wind (or the drama?) safely from indoors. The personification of the wind and of the tree and the sense of conflict between the two is typical (see Aesop's fable of the Wind and the Sun):

I can hear the dogs barking
down at the seaside.
The waves howling.
The water hits
      the pebbles,
whistling when it slides
back into the sea.
The storm wind blows
Through the trees.
One of the trees is
down with a thumping
noise. And the branches
rattle their twigs because
they are angry.

Julie Floyd (Wellington, Somerset)

In the following poem the wind spreads confusion, and one is not, as in the previous poem, made to feel the mighty power of the elements, but rather the nagging disruption to ordinary things. Fluff (the dog or cat, or perhaps dandelion 'clocks'?), the calendar, the tins and papers, are all affected. But most of all one is conscious of the structure of this poem. The line lengths and the repetitions emphasize the variety of the rhythms. The longer lines

The wind   the wind makes you cold
Listen   listen to the wind

give the effect of a continuous force, while in

The car goes swoosh
Along the road
Tins and papers
Make noises

we feel the sudden gusts. In the second verse the line structure emphasizes a new rhythm suited to the steady, rock-like character of Old McWilliam:

Blowing
Blow away
Wind
I feel shivery and frightened

Fluff flies in and tearing
The calendar
It makes you freeze
Blow Blow away home
The wind　the wind makes you cold
Listen　listen to the wind
It makes you cold
I feel frozen
The car goes swoosh
Along the road
Tins and papers
Make noises
The wind makes a noise
Like this　whoo
Old McWilliam will be cold
Because he is outside a lot
Doing the roadside He leaves
His bicycle in our turnip
shed sometimes　I think it is
in our shed just now
But he gets a lift home
with a lorry sometimes
Then he is lucky

David Morrison (Wigtown)

The next poem shows an understanding of the cycle of life for predatory animals with man as the final predator. The drama of the chain of events is heightened by the night, the atmosphere being set in the first four words, 'The night doth fall'. (The archaism is surely justified in this instance, for its soft sound and the air of mystery which is at once established.)

The night doth fall　and out every
Little mouse peeps one comes out
And then all　but　alas! alas!　they all
Go into the littlest hole they find

Screech　Screech　a big screech owl
Comes but O the clever owl
Its eyes peep　and a big fat rat
For dinner　what a feast

It has   but alas!   alas!   a big fat
Fox wanted his dinner and growling
Softly to itself

The owl eats the mouse the
Fox eats the owl and in a shoot
The fox is dead with a bang
And it is gone.

Bruce MacRae (Fife)

The next example of infants' free writing is no less remarkable than the last for its intuitive feeling for rhythm. If one reads the first verse aloud, stressing the beat in certain consecutive lines, one realizes that the cuckoo's cry goes on and on and on, sometimes with the briefest pause as a change of accent sees a new pattern of the same sound:

'Cuckoo   Cuckoo   Cuckoo   Cuckoo'
That's the cuckoo's voice I say
It is   It is   It is.   That's the
cuckoo,   that is the cuckoo's
voice   I know   I know   it is

The sound is immediate, the words and the meaning adapt themselves to it. The same consideration may be applied to the verse with the cymbals, with its hint of a marching rhythm, but whereas it becomes increasingly clear that, in a sense, the child *becomes* the cuckoo by imitating it, he is able to stand outside the percussive noise and regard it as an enemy, albeit a fascinating enemy:

When I hear the cuckoo I
Know it is spring. 'Cuckoo
Cuckoo   Cuckoo'   I don't know why I
Like that noise, but I like
That sharp high note, that says
'Cuckoo   Cuckoo   Cuckoo   Cuckoo'
That's the cuckoo's voice I say,
It is   It is   It is.   That's the
cuckoo, that is the cuckoo's
voice   I know   I know   it is

I don't like the noise that
the cymbals make   it is a bit
too loud for me.   Clang clang
clang clang. What a loud
noise that is   Clang clang   oh dear
what a deafening noise   oh dear,
bang clang clang bang   what
a terrible din   oh dear   oh
dear.

Margaret Still (Aberdeen)

In most cases there is a break with at least a possibility of regression when children enter the junior school, and it is realistic at this stage to assume that experiences and occasions for writing need to be organized in some way, particularly at first. Moreover, due to special circumstances, some teachers may find themselves introducing creative writing as a new experience in the junior or even the secondary school.

We should make it clear that we see little value in children's attempts at metrical verse at least until the later stages in the secondary school, and even there it is likely that the results will compare unfavourably with sincere emotional expression with un-rhymed verse written in the 'natural' rhythms of speech and thought. If creative writing has to be introduced after writing in prose has been firmly established, it is wise to give the children a taste of adult writers of free verse, and of other children's writing in that form.

The chief resistances to creative writing after the infant stage are the fear of failure, which frequently arises from an over-anxiety to avoid 'mistakes'; a misconception that poetry must obey strict 'rules' (those followed in almost all the poetry that young children meet); and a distrust of the feelings, which sometimes goes with an obsession for factual information. The remedy for these misgivings lies with the teacher, who will be concerned to build up an attitude of encouragement and discussion rather than one of correction. With older children, particularly, it is sometimes better to discuss a poem with the writer before reading it aloud to the class; and occasionally, in the case of highly personal writing, it is better not to read it publicly.

It is important that some success is achieved at the first attempt, and for that reason, as a short term measure only, it may be worth while to organize the making of a group poem. One method is for the teacher to decide on some focal point for the class's attention – something concrete is probably best, an 'object' selected for its power of evoking wider associations. The stimulus should not be something that can be immediately identified and labelled, but rather something that can excite curiosity. An interesting piece of drift-wood, or a miscellaneous collection of large stones, can be handled as well as looked at; other objects may have a 'life' of their own – bubbles can rise and burst, feathers can float in the air. During the experience words and phrases will either arise spontaneously, or as the result of carefully directed questions. This is where the teacher's own imagination is called into play.

To take the example of the driftwood – with the teacher 'directing' the children's observation – the following reconstruction illustrates the possible sequence. The driftwood is held up where the children can all see it, handled sensitively, and perhaps put down on a table cleared of everything else. The talking begins ... In discussion it be-comes apparent that the driftwood has colour and texture. It has weight, perhaps heavier, perhaps lighter, than we would expect (a child may be asked to 'try' it) ... It has shape, it is hard, it emits a particular sound when tapped ... (At each point in the observation words and phrases will come from the class perhaps, though not necessarily, prompted by the teacher's questions. These may be collected and recorded. ... Now the driftwood may be turned round and looked at from different angles. Perhaps it reminds us of some-thing else ... (Thus the teacher may steer the response on to a deeper level of imagination.) ... It is old. It has been exposed to the elements ... if it were a hundred times its present size ... (But before this point, perhaps the class has taken the initiative and ideas are coming from *them*).

It is obvious that a group poem could be made from an arrange-ment of the children's language responses to the experience of the driftwood; but, on the other hand, individual poems may be attemp-ted, perhaps on a parallel line to avoid direct recall of the phrases used in the discussion. It is always best to begin creative writing from a new viewpoint.

Experiences of the kind that we have described cannot *give* the children language, but they can release language which would otherwise remain at an unconscious level, so that it can be shared and appreciated in a wider context. The resulting 'poem' will probably be limited by a lack of development and uneven through its self-conscious determination to include a wide variety of ideas, but it will invariably contain some colourful phrases which touch the children's imagination. Most important at this stage is the sense of achievement shared by all the children.

Sometimes one may wish to concentrate attention on a single sense to the exclusion of the rest. The senses of hearing and of touch may be sharpened by closing the eyes, and it is very simple within the classroom to organize experiences of that kind. The right atmosphere, serious but not solemn, is of course essential, but that is a matter for the teacher's personality to establish, and normally junior children are very eager or willing to participate as in a kind of game (and nothing is more serious than a game).

It is not suggested that writing should always accompany experiments like this one, though discussion always will. Sometimes, in fact, it is better to defer the writing, or to introduce it in connection with a new experience. It is not always reasonable to expect an immediate reaction which will produce language of quality, and language of a more original character may result when children have had time to digest the experience, and perhaps to select the particular features which they want to use. Sometimes the transfer is more remote, but of greater value on that account, as it shows that the experience has been more fully assimilated.

The time will soon come when some children, at least, will be ready to try and make poems of their own. For the time being, perhaps, a stimulus will be necessary, and at other times experiments in sound-making and listening (a tape-recorder is most useful here) in movement and drama, and in painting, will contribute to the same creative stream. A background of music sometimes produces a flow of imaginative ideas which may be expressed in writing or in art.

Sometimes with young children a very simple lead may be given, perhaps a phrase or an unfinished sentence which may be patterned by the children into a poem. The following are examples which have proved successful in starting children on creative writing:

I can hear...
I like ...

I can see...
I wish I had..

It is sufficient to say that once the ice is broken, poems will flow in great measure. The Plowden Report noted, in fact, that the amount and quality of children's writing was 'Perhaps the most dramatic of all revolutions in English teaching'. Here there is no shortage of subjects, as there was in the days of the old weekly 'composition'. Children sometimes write about their own personal experiences, but often more effectively about their fantasies – the power of the elements (the giants in the winds, in storms at sea, in earthquakes), prehistoric monsters, noises in the night, the mystery of quiet, deserted places, fears and expressions of love.

We have grouped our examples of creative writing and poetry in the junior school to suggest the kind of framework in which the writing was conceived. This classification is to some extent arbitrary, but as teachers we inevitably see our children's activities in relation to the classroom. One of the most obvious ways of creating atmosphere is to change the light by some means or other. This is done most dramatically in the following poem :

CANDLELIGHT · Caroline Dawson, aged 10

Tucked away in the dark
We looked at the candle flame.
Wisps of coloured light
And tiny pools of wax
Surrounded by a deep blue candle.

Our eyes sparkled and glinted
As the coloured lights met them,
With its blues and golds, yellows and browns
Glowing in darkness
As if it were night-time.

Hair seemed to be tinted
And shoes so highly polished,
All this mingled with a flame,
A flame coming from a blue candle
Being held by a shining hand.

It is obvious that the stimulus was powerful enough to evoke effective images of colour, light and shade. The writer, at ten years of age, is highly competent to select from a wide range of words the precise verb or adjective most appropriate to express what she clearly *sees*. In addition, at the beginning one notices an intuitive feeling for the simple, direct statement which falls pleasantly on the ear. In contrast, there is perhaps a feeling of banality in the reference to the hair and the shoes; but that may be inevitable when the child is so close to the experience that she fails to reject what is irrelevant to the creation in her poem. More important is the final image which, for the child, is the enduring symbol associated with the experience – the flame ... held by a shining hand. Nevertheless, it might be felt that the poem is a piece of descriptive rather than imaginative writing. Another child, in response to a similar stimulus elsewhere, wrote:

> *The burning flame of spears,*
> *The quicksand drying up,*
> *The smoke signal of Red Indians,*
> *The melting of white icicles.*

The first child has been faithful to the experience and the second has reached beyond it, but any attempt to evaluate one in relation to the other on grounds of 'vocabulary' or 'relevance' would obviously be pointless.

The next poem begins with the child looking at a stone. If his attention had not been engaged by the object the poem would never have been written:

THOUSANDS OF DROPS ON A STONE ·
Riaz Hussain, aged 10

> *Thousands of years ago*
> *In a cave deep down below,*
> *A drop of water fell on a stone.*
> *Drop after drop of water fell on that stone*
> *Till gradually a bit of the stone wore away*
> *To find part of the stone as smooth as amber.*
>
> *Thousands of years ago*
> *In a cave deep down below,*

> *Some smells of lime water seeped into that stone*
> *And after some time these mysterious smells*
> *Lingered into the mysterious stone.*

It is not flawless, of course, for very few children's poems are, but its qualities of sensitivity to the sound of language far outweigh the occasional awkwardness of phrasing. The writer has an innate feeling for form and balance in rhythm, and within the structure contrasts of sound and movement give each verse its distinctive character. For example, the word 'drop', repeated as it is in the first verse, has a life of its own, suggesting regularity of sound and movement; on the other hand, the words *smells, steeped, mysterious* and *lingered* have a different quality of sound and movement, and (perhaps because of associations with the first word) of taste. The effect of the rhymed couplet at the beginning of each verse is almost hypnotic.

Experiments in sound-making in the classroom have already been mentioned, and these no doubt served to focus the next writer's attention on distinctive qualities of sound. Here the technique of listening has been applied to a sophisticated appraisal of the rest of humanity gathered together in a cinema, between one film and the next:

THE CINEMA · Child, aged 11

> *Crunching, munching of Smith's crisps,*
> *The little woosh as a match is lit,*
> *Music on the film,*
> *Money clanging in the ice-cream box.*
> *Can I have two tubs please?*
> *That's one and six dear.*
> *The mumbling of people talking*
> *Giving their views on the film,*
> *The soft thudding of people's feet*
> *Walking up the aisle.*
> *The little boy next to me starts crying*
> *His mother is frantically trying to make him quiet.*
> *Eventually he stops,*
> *And I settle back to watch the film.*

In a similarly detached view of the colour, noise and movement of the outside world, the writer of the next poem stands outside the experience as a commentator (compare some of the examples in Chapter 4 of the various points of view). But he seems to write with authority about what he does know, the rush and squalor of a modern city:

NEW YORK CITY · Philip Bertelli, aged 10

People chatting and babies crying,
Auto buses honking,
With huge cars sweeping up behind,
And drivers shouting their curses
Upon slow push-bikes.

Small and snug little shops
Full of toys and sweet candy.

There are some children crouching
Around toy shops,
And some crying out
For ice-cream outside the drug-stores.
Buildings with a hundred storeys.
Oh! What a life in New York City.

The next poem is by an adult writer, but it seems to fit in the context of this chapter. It is an evocation of sounds, movement and colour in a fantasy world which is both exciting and real to many junior children. It is a splendid poem to read aloud and, though we have never used it in this way, it would surely stimulate a variety of activities; again it could be seen as relevant in a variety of topics – Speed, Red Indians, Noise, Trains, to mention a few.

THE WIND AT NIGHT · David Shavreen

The dustbin lids clang on the ground,
The treetops groan,
The wind down the bedroom chimney
Begins to moan.
I hear a sudden roar
Through the blankets covering my face,

The clatter and rattle of wheels
At a furious pace;
It's the Union Express, the Iron Steed,
Rumbling across the prairies
At breakneck speed.

It pounds through the chimney stacks.
Screams to a halt,
Stops in its tracks.

Silence follows.
Then with a hiss
The airy train
Accelerates again,
Thundering along the housetops
With shrieks and bellows.
Racing across the Plains
It splashes through mud and mire,
Outstripping the painted Redskins,
Their arrows fierce as fire;
Outwitting the train-wreckers,
Men masked and mean with greed,
With a fierce burst of steam
And a triumphant rattle of speed.
And the Indians wail and howl
Raising their cry of despair
As the rear-lamp swings into darkness,
And the train melts into air.

And the bandits shout their curses
After their vanished prey,
Till the oaths echo around the roofs
And the thudding of horses' hoofs
Flying, dying away
Grows still, and silence deep
At last brings calm
And sleep.

The two train poems which follow were both written by boys in the same class. They are widely different. In *The Engine Shed* there is a sophistication in the vocabulary and in the use of half-rhymes which is unusual for an eleven-year-old. But, more important, there is a close involvement and sense of nostalgia for an age which is rapidly passing. He takes an historical view which could perhaps be paralleled in a study of other things in the past. *The Underground* is, by contrast, immediate and modern:

THE ENGINE SHED · Boy, aged 11

I would like to go and see
engines, steam engines,
large and small, all sizes,
hissing from their whistles,
blowing clouds of steam from their chimneys,
their great wheels slowly turning
their huge buffers gradually demolishing
a brick wall, blackened by years of being
subjected to spurts of steam, clouds of steam
forced out by countless engines of their boilers.

The windows, mostly smashed,
bare peepholes for enthusiasts,
while themselves they've seen
all engines from the age of steam.
How quiet then seems the sleeping yard,
the engines motionless, scratched and marred,
the wheels which pulled the express
now in their turn have come to rest.

In *The Underground*, the poem which follows, words and images have been carefully assembled to create the contrast between the brilliant, staccato effect of flashing light and the dull, heavy atmosphere in the world above. The human beings appropriately are nameless automata, as they are in some of the Ministry of Transport's current rush-hour posters. In the first five lines the medley of sound, movement and colour sets the scene on the waiting platform. The confusion of the mass exodus of the 'prisoners' is well contrasted with the air of precision in movement with which, like clockwork, the commuters are emptied into the street. Parallels in music are not difficult to find, and we are particularly reminded of the opening of

William Walton's Façade Suite. The children could create in drama
or in other media their own idea of this world:

THE UNDERGROUND · Boy, aged 11

Rattling, clattering, grumbling and moaning,
The train emerges from the black tunnel,
Showering sharp blue sparks,
In welcome to the brightly lit terminus.
Then glides noisily in beside the platform,
Brakes scraping harshly on the bright rails.

A short hush,
Then doors slide back in fright,
To let their seething prisoners out
Of the thick musty vapour,
Onto the platform with bruised feet and sore elbows
Amidst myriads, galaxies of indication lights,
*   posters and slot machines.*
The chill air blows down
As the escalator purrs upwards,
Taking its load of assorted humanity,
To the ticket office located above.
There their tickets are snicked,
And they briskly stride out,
Into the fogbound street.

For some teachers and some classes writing can happily arise from
everyday situations in the classroom. In the particular school in
North London from which the following poems come, the strong
sense of community and the philosophic humour is fostered in the
multi-racial society of the neighbourhood.

P.E. · D. Pollard, aged 10

First when you come in the hall
You curl like a cat
You run, then you jump
Like a kangaroo.
I stretch, I curl, I jump
I do backward rolls or forward rolls

F

Headstands   elbowstands   handstands
Coming down there backrolls or forward rolls
I attack the apparatus
I twist, I curl, I stretch on the ropes
I jump up like a tiger to a beam
         Then I fall
              Soft, soft landing
           Like a bird.

THE JUMBLE SALE · Girl, aged 10

Just a penny for this
Luscious old cardigan, Ma'am.
No! Don't buy his
Awful old trash (from the dustpan).
Look at this
Superb botany bed-socks,
A very good bargain Missus
For fivepence.
I look around
What awful trash!
But listen to the jangle of that money! Eh.

SHOES · Andrew, aged 9

One shoe was ... b-bad,
Me!   The shoe with no lace,
Holes!   no thread, useless and bedraggled.
Kicked, bitten, trodden on,
By my brothers and ancestors.
If I was made again, polished,
I would be happy.
My mother was stabbed for thread
Sixteen times,
She didn't yell, she couldn't speak;
Her tongue was stitched.

Compassion and a sense of wonder is perhaps the deepest quality that can be found in children's writing. One cannot doubt that all

the children concerned in the following poems were deeply moved
by their subjects. The first is by an eight-year-old boy. Commentary
here seems hardly necessary, but the writer may have met Blake's
poem *The Tiger* and sought to imitate it;

THE TIGER · Boy, aged 8

The Tiger prowls
Through the dark
Stricken night.
Nothing in sight.
He strolls along
With his gleaming
Eyes, the terrible
Tiger, yellow and black.
Everything soundless.
Here it comes the
Tiger. Here comes the
Tiger through the dark
Perilous night.
The grass shivers in
The night.
A fear of terror
Struck a roamer
Walking through the
Soundless grass.
Here comes the tiger,
Here comes the tiger,
Through the dark, stricken night.

In writing an elegy on the death of her pet the next writer
establishes two levels in distancing the tragedy. The lyrical beginning
and ending may have been inspired by the musical reading of her
teacher, herself a lover of poetry; the agonized outburst in the
middle of the poem suggests that the pain has not been entirely
exorcized:

SPARKEY · Janice Colledge, aged 9

When the lanes are wrapped in twilight
And the Autumn leaves float down like red gold

Then I remember her.
Her amber eyes
And I can't believe that we played and chased
She lies buried,
A little heap of stones – to remind me – as if I'd forget
Drivers – reckless people
Not all of them
Why was it her?
She was so beautiful
So aloft and haughty
Perhaps people have felt this way before
No doubt they have
But again I ask   Why me?   Why me?
She was so silky to touch
And sleek
I shouldn't feel bitter
But I do
Her basket is empty now
Just a cat   just a cat
But I loved her
When the lanes are wrapped in twilight
And the Autumn leaves float down like red gold
Then I remember her
Sparkey.

The next, by a ten-year-old boy, is full of sadness at the transitory quality of life, especially for tiny things. It is admirably economical and exact in its use of language. Every adjective and every noun makes its individual impact; those dealing with the present, as most do, are contrasted with those of the past – *alive, plumes, feathers,* with *brittle, hard, eerie* and so on:

THE SKULL OF A BIRD · Gabriel Ellenberg, aged 10

Delicate and hard,
Tiny and fragile,
Eerie and brittle.
Skull of a minute bird
Once alive with plumes and feathers,
Now nothing but bone.

A sad air hangs about it,
Little brittle skull.

If the last poem was a still life, the next is a landscape. The stillness and the silence are of a different quality but they are both
present in the prose poem; they are waiting to be broken. The
images of life and death have a unity as well as an antithesis within
the poem. In common with the others in this selection of com-
passionate poems, the question 'Why?' is implicit. Here it is urgent
and, the writer believes, should not be forgotten:

> *The quiet drone of a bee, an almost silent whisper of breeze*
> *across the icy water make the world an almost desolate place.*
> *The rustle of reeds that conceal the silent moorhen as she*
> *dips her shining crimson body in the ice blue water. No more*
> *do the soldiers run, no more does death befall them, as it did*
> *in days of old.*
> *But all now is forgotten as we admire the country they fought*
> *for in their livelihood.*
> *And even now I watch and listen at the beauties of this*
> *earth, what made them fight, what made them die?*
> *A perch breaks the shining water. Does he know the cries*
> *that broke the air? And does he know the sweetness of the*
> *earth? I wonder. The robin perches on a bough and sings his*
> *sweet chorus, like the drums and fifes of a splendid army. A*
> *bang sounds and a rook falls; the farmer has claimed a victim.*
> *With bloodstained breast he falls silent to the ground. Splash!*
> *an otter hits the water with the force of immense power that*
> *distils and breaks the peacefulness of the day, like a dead*
> *soldier falling into a waterlogged trench.*
>
> David Pomroy, aged 11

Too much comment on this would be superfluous, but we might
ponder momentarily on the area of awareness explored by a child
in language which fixes immutably the poignant and ever-present
problems of our own time.

7

Conclusion

STRICTLY, there is no conclusion to this brief guide to the use of
poetry with children and the multiple experiences it provides for
them and for us, the teachers. Poetry can be mysterious, mystical,
fulfilling, tantalizing; by analogy, exploring his imagination, a child
has said it all for us:

CHEST · Michael Rawlings, aged 11

I seek a chest that
lies in wait for someone
to feel the feel
of slimy seaweed.

I seek a chest that lies
silently for someone
to fear in the
dark and hushing waves.

I seek a chest
that
submerges when the tide floods.

I seek a chest that fills
me full of excitement
when the limpets
cling to it.

A chest that holds the key to all of the
excitement in my life and when I
open the chest I feel
like dancing, singing

but the chest
is not there for my dreams
to have joy.

In a live classroom there is always something meaningful happening, and in this case we are fortunate enough to have an insight into the creative stimulus from the teacher herself. She writes:

> Michael produced his poem during a project on 'The Sea', which we covered in Geography and Science, as well as in English. To encourage the imaginative writing of poems and stories the children made a treasure chest, from an old orange box, and filled it with beads, brooches etc. At the time Sir Francis Chichester was on his round the Horn trip. This we followed closely, and poems were written about *Gypsy Moth* and pictures painted.

And in the earlier poem quoted in the last chapter (*Skull of a Dead Bird*) we have a parent's testimony as to the quality of the teaching her son received. Mrs. Ellenberg tells us that the late Miss Margaret Flynn gave her sons 'the impetus to write', and we feel, and indeed have stressed throughout this book, that this impetus lies within the gift of the positive teacher. The sense of fulfilment in writing which we have seen in younger children is by no means lacking in children of secondary age, as the following examples show:

A BLACK AND WHITE EVENING PHOTOGRAPH ·

Clouds spreading
Like a smooth patchwork over the sky,
The sky that covers, covers everything.
Leaning and leaning and leaning until it
Compresses the beyond into
The thin thread of the horizon.
Dark recognised shapes are fretsawed
Out of this quiet painting.
Movement is an excuse for dying.
Anything that need not be done
Today, need never be done.   Anthony Harpur, (Form I)

The aged man looked down
Down on his family tree, but
At the bottom a medieval monkey looked down
On something much better than a tree
A sixpence.

John Moon, (Form II)

The cat lay as though in ecstacy
watching with fancy
his dictator who struts
with a grand posture.
Set high above his prominent nose
on his balcony
alone –
alone with his virginity,
his sentiment
his retirement . . .
and his cat.

Thomas Clough, (Form IV)

Here in all three poems the unique individual quality of the imagination is shown; whether it is an attitude, a moment, a flake of wit or the charging of words with associations way beyond their definitions, each of these poems bears the indelible stamp of its creator. And it is the stamp, if you like, which each teacher of poetry has to offer the children she teaches. Today so many of our words have synthetic rather than real meanings, and one of our tasks as teachers is to show the real in positive relief against the false. For the teacher who responds to poetry, and for the child who listens, reads and perhaps creates areas of experience for herself and others, the reality exists in the imagination of the poet.

Bibliography

THE books listed below have been classified as follows:

1 Reading for the teacher.
2 Anthologies for the classroom library with which the teacher should be familiar, these are marked as a guide to their suitability for different children – *a*, suitable for infant and lower junior school pupils; *b*, suitable for upper junior school children; *c*, suitable for secondary school children.
3 Poets' collections (categorized *a*, *b* and *c* as group 2).
4 Collections of children's writing.

The list has been compiled as a guide, but obviously teachers will read widely themselves – particularly modern poetry, we hope – and they will make their own lists as a result of their reading.

1   Reading for the teacher

BLACKBURN, T. (Ed.). *Presenting Poetry*. Methuen, 1966.

CLEGG, A. B. (Ed.). *The Excitement of Writing*. Chatto and Windus, 1964.

DRUCE, R. *The Eye of Innocence*. Second Edition University of London Press, 1970.

FORD, BORIS. (Ed.). *Young Writers, Young Readers*. Hutchinson, 1963.

HOURD, M. L. and COOPER, G. E. *Coming into Their Own*. Heinemann Educational, 1959.

MARSHALL, S. *Experiment in Education*. Cambridge, 1963.

MAYBURY, B. *Creative Writing for Juniors*. Batsford, 1967.

MORRIS, H., *Where's That Poem?* Blackwell, 1967.

PEEL, M. *Seeing to the Heart*. Chatto and Windus, 1967.

2   *Anthologies for the classroom*

BALDWIN, M. (Ed.). *Billy the Kid*. Hutchinson, 1963. *c*.

BERG, L. (Ed.). *Four Feet and Two*. Puffin Series. Penguin, 1960. *a,b*.

BLISHEN, E. (Ed.). *Oxford Book of Poetry for Children*. Oxford, 1963.
b.

BRITTON, J. (Ed.). *The Oxford Book of Verse for Juniors*. Oxford,
1957. *b*.

CAUSLEY, C. *Dawn and Dusk*. Brockhampton, 1962. *b,c*.

CAUSLEY, C. *Rising Early*. Brockhampton, 1964. *b,c*.

CLARK, LEONARD (Ed.). *Common Ground*. Faber, new edition 1966.
b.

CLARK, LEONARD *Daybreak*. Hart-Davies, 1963. *a*.

CLARK, LEONARD (Ed.). *Drums and Trumpets*. Bodley Head, 1962.
a,b.

CLARK, LEONARD (Ed.). *Flutes and Cymbals*. Bodley Head, 1968. *b*.

GIBSON, J. and WILSON, R. (Ed.). *Rhyme and Rhythm*. Macmillan,
1965. *b*.

GRAHAM, ELEANOR (Ed.). *The Puffin Book of Verse*. Penguin, 1953. *b*.

GRAHAM, ELEANOR (Ed.). *Secret Laughter*. Penguin, 1969. *b*.

GRAHAM, ELEANOR (Ed.). *A Puffin Quartet of Poets*. Penguin, 1958.
(The four poets are Eleanor Farjeon, E. V. Rieu, James Reeves and
Ian Serriallier.) *b*.

HEWETT, S. (Ed.). *This Day and Age*. Arnold, 1960. *c*.

HOLBROOK, D. (Ed.). *Iron, Honey and Gold*. Cambridge. 1965. *c*.

HUGHES, TED (Ed.) *Here Today*. Hutchinson, 1963. *c*.

MACBAIN, I. M. (Ed.). *Come Follow Me*. Evans, new edition 1966. *a,b*.

MANSFIELD, R. and ARMSTRONG, I. (Ed.). *Every Man Will Shout*. Oxford, 1964. *c*.

OPIE, I. and OPIE, P. (Ed.). *Puffin Book of Nursery Rhymes*. Puffin
Series. Penguin, 1967. *a,b*.

REEVES, J. (Ed.). *The Merry-Go-Round*. Puffin Series. Penguin, 1967.
a,b.

SERGEANT, H. *The Swinging Rainbow*. Evans, 1969. *a,b*.

SHAW, R. (Ed.). *Flash Point*. Arnold, 1964. *c*.

SMITH, J. A. (Ed.). *The Faber Book of Children's Verse*. Faber, 1953. *b*.

SMITH, W. J. (Ed.). *The Golden Journey*. Evans, 1967. *b*.

STEVENSON, R. L. *A Child's Garden of Verses*. Bodley Head, 1960.
Also in Puffin Series by Penguin. *a,b*.

SUMMERFIELD, G. *Voices*. Books 1, 2 and 3. Penguin, 1968. *c*.

WOLLMAN, M. and GRUGEON, D. (Ed.). *Happenings*. Harrap, 1964. *b*, *c*.

3 Poet's Collections

BELLOC, HILAIRE. *Selected Cautionary Verses* (includes *A Bad Child's Book of Beasts*) Puffin Series. Penguin, 1950. *b*.
BLAKE, WILLIAM. *A Grain of Sand*. Bodley Head, 1967. *b,c*.
CAUSLEY, CHARLES. *Figures of Eight*. Macmillan, 1969. *b,c*.
CLARE, JOHN. *The Wood is Sweet*. Bodley Head, 1966. *b.c*.
DE LA MARE, WALTER. *Peacock Pie*. Faber, 1941. New Edition, 1953. *b*.
ELIOT, T. S. *Old Possum's Book of Practical Cats*. Faber, 1953. *b*.
FARJEON, ELEANOR. *The Children's Bells: Poems*. Oxford, 1957. *b*.
FROST, ROBERT. *You Come Too*. Bodley Head, 1964. *b,c*.
GRAVES, ROBERT. *Ann at Highwood Hall*. Cassell, 1964. *b*.
HUGHES, TED. (Ed.). *Meet My Folks*. Faber, 1964. *b*.
HUGHES, TED. *Nessie the Mannerless Monster*. Faber, 1964. *b*.
JACKSON, H. (Ed.). *The Complete Nonsense of Edward Lear*. Faber, 1947. *b*.
MILLIGAN, SPIKE. *Silly Verse for Kids*. Dobson, 1963. Also in Puffin Series by Penguin. *b*.
NASH, OGDEN. *Parents Keep Out*. Dent, 1962. *b,c*.
REEVES, JAMES. *Blackbird in Lilac*. Oxford, 1952. *b*.
REEVES, JAMES. *Prefabulous Animiles*. Heinemann, 1957. *b*.
SANSOM, CLIVE. *Return to Magic*. Frewin, 1969. *b*.
SERAILLIER, IAN. *Beowulf the Warrior*. Oxford, 1954. *b*.
SERAILLIER, IAN. *Robin in the Green Wood*. Oxford, 1967. *b*.
WALSH, JOHN. *The Roundabout by the Sea*. Oxford, 1960. *b*.

4 Children's Writing

Children as Writers. Daily Mirror, annual publication.
CAHIN, M. and LLOYD, J. (Ed.). *From a Busy Hubbub*. Collins, 1969.
LEWIS, R. (Ed.). *Miracles*. Allen Lane The Penguin Press, 1967.

NOTE: The Gramophone *Spoken Word Catalogue* gives a comprehensive list of poetry on record.

Index

Poets quoted or mentioned are listed here. Other writers mentioned in the text are listed in the *Bibliography* (pages 89–91). *Nursery Rhymes* and traditional verses will be found on pages 27–36, 56–7, 58 and in the index of first lines. *Children's Writing* is listed under a separate index of first lines.

Authors

Index of First Lines or Titles

Children's Writing – Index of First Lines
Titles are included where given.